D0779566

Reaching Godward

VOICES FROM

JEWISH SPIRITUAL GUIDANCE

Also by Carol Ochs:
_____

Our Lives as Torah: Finding God in Our Own Stories

Jewish Spiritual Guidance: Finding Our Way to God
(with Kerry M. Olitzky)

Paths of Faithfulness: Personal Essays on Jewish Spirituality
(joint editor)

Song of the Self: Biblical Spirituality and Human Holiness

The Noah Paradox: Time as Burden, Time as Blessing

An Ascent to Joy: Transforming Deadness of Spirit

Women and Spirituality

*Behind the Sex of God: Toward a New Consciousness
Transcending Matriarchy and Patriarchy*

Reaching Godward

VOICES FROM JEWISH SPIRITUAL GUIDANCE

CAROL OCHS

URJ Press   •   New York, New York

Library of Congress Cataloging-in-Publication Data

Ochs, Carol.
    Reaching Godward : voices from Jewish spiritual guidance / Carol
Ochs.
        p.   cm.
    ISBN 0-8074-0866-2 (pbk. : alk. paper)
    1. Spiritual life—Judaism—Case studies.   2. Jewish way of life—Case
Studies.   I. Title.
    BM723.037   2004
    296.6′1—dc22
                                                                                    2004005100

This book is printed on acid-free paper.
Copyright © 2004 by Carol Ochs.
Manufactured in the United States of America.

10   9   8   7   6   5   4   3   2   1

To Sheila Hammond,
Theresa Brophy, and Dorothy Murray—
spiritual guides, teachers, friends

I give all my guidees two simple rules:

1. Whatever is said in this room stays in this room.

2. You set the agenda.

Contents

Preface   xi

Introduction   1

1. Deena   *Bringing a Love of Dance into Worship*   11

2. Dorothy   *Dealing with Aging*   22

3. David   *Mourning a Stillborn Daughter*   38

4. Stanley   *A Psychologist Explores Spiritual Guidance*   49

5. Eli   *The Meaning of Loneliness within the Family*   68

6. Paul   *A Philosopher on His Deathbed Reexamines His Work*   90

7. Florence   *Understanding the Creative Process*   99

8. Rachel   *A Teacher Explores Her Spiritual Commitment*   118

9. Glynis   *An Adult Daughter's Reconciliation with Her Mother*   128

10. Laura   *A Mother "Releasing" Her Grown Daughter*   140

11. Martin   *A Priest Discusses a Personal Problem*   156

12. Pauline   *An Attorney Struggles with a Biblical Text*   163

13. Sarah   *A Marriage and the Healing of Childhood Losses*   180

14. Joan   *A Young Guidee Returns as a Social Worker*   191

15. Marion   *The Gift of Creativity That Saves a Marriage*   208

16. Maureen   *Remaining a Jew-by-Choice after the Children Are Grown*   219

Afterword   233

Preface

Just after my seventeenth birthday, while attending a summer session class at the University of Wisconsin, I experienced a moment of such transcendent recognition, homecoming, and profound joy that—then and there—I presumed my vocation had been sealed for life. I had just read Plato for the first time. I realized then that the thoughts I'd been having all my life were not bizarre, as I had assumed. Since early childhood, it seemed, I had been telling myself that there must be more to life than the world I could see, hear, and touch. I had wondered how I could get at it, how to explain it. I knew only that I yearned for it. And finally I discovered that there was a whole discipline dealing with such issues, and it was called philosophy.

Socrates, whose ideas Plato expounds, put a human face on a life dedicated to reminding the citizens of Athens that their greatest task lay in tending their souls. As I continued my study of philosophy, only one other philosopher exhibited to me such devotion, such exemplary behavior, such truth—Baruch de Spinoza. For twenty-five years I was content to teach philosophy of religion, philosophy of mind, metaphysics, and specialized courses within these fields, trying to awaken my students' awareness to the reality and value of their souls.

And then, sitting in my study one bright, wintry day, I had another memorable experience.

In my doctoral thesis, I had explored the ontological proof for the existence of God, as found in the writings of Descartes, Spinoza, and Leibnitz. The ontological argument is an exercise in logic that "proves" the existence of God by saying that essence entails existence. Or put another way: if we can assume a being—God—no greater than which can be conceived, then that being must exist, because existence is greater than nonexistence. I had been introduced to the ontological proof ten years earlier, during that summer at Wisconsin, and its beauty and self-sufficiency had taken my breath away. But that day in my study, while contemplating the ontological proof once again, I sensed that I was being invited to know in my heart what I had known through reason and in my mind. I then recalled a line by John D. Sinclair in his commentary on Dante's *Paradiso*: "The scholastic, by faithfulness to reason, became the mystic." All I had to do was assent. God, whom I regarded as the source and guarantor of truth, meaning, and value, was also one with whom I could be in a personal relationship.

Not all our sages and other thinkers subscribe to the ontological proof. Maimonides offered proofs for the existence of God but did not employ the ontological argument. Spinoza did, however, and from it derived his highest good, "the intellectual love of God." I had read these words and taught them over and over again in seminars on Spinoza, but only when I started seeing them with the emphasis changed did they leap off the page: the intellectual *love* of God. Nothing is negated, nothing discarded, but now the journey of reason had taken me to a place far beyond what reason could posit.

We are not our own ends—our being and well-being point to a larger whole, of which we are only a part. Reason, similarly, is not its own end; it invites us to a larger vision that takes up reason into a larger whole. I continue to teach Spinoza and I continue to love Plato, but now I know that the greatest good lies in each of us recognizing, claiming, and entering into our own relationship with God.

One of my goals in pursuing spiritual guidance is to help people find their own paths to understanding their purpose in life—to be fully themselves, by helping them find God in their lives. Some of the people I work with in spiritual guidance are rationalists, as I am. And while, recently, there has been a trend to forego reason in search of "true" intimacy with God, I have never suggested that a guidee deny reason in seeking such a relationship. Reason is one of the gifts we have been given, and in fully employing these gifts, we come to experience the giver.

Out of this intimate experience we often discover just what it is we are called to do. I am continually awed—and humbled—by the unending variety of ways God calls to us and invites us into relationship. When Socrates heard the Delphic Oracle proclaim him to be the wisest man in Athens, he—knowing that he *lacked* wisdom—set out to discover what passed as wisdom in his society. That quest, he claimed, became the impetus behind his search for the meaning of piety, truth, justice, beauty, and the good. His experience became his calling. Similarly, once I became aware that God was not simply the God of reason and of tradition, but One to whom we could relate in this unique, all-encompassing sense, it became clear to me that my experience was, in fact, my calling to help others develop *their* personal relationships with God.

I warmly appreciate the support of Ken Gesser, publisher of the URJ Press, and of Rabbi Hara Person, editorial director of the Press. Hara's encouragement, dedication, and excellent editorial suggestions did much to improve the book. I also thank URJ Press staff members Liane Broido, Debra Hirsch Corman, Michael Goldberg, Annie Belford, and Joel Eglash for their contributions to producing and marketing the volume. My deepest gratitude goes to my daughter, Lisa Ochs, a compassionate nurse and an extraordinary book doctor, who helped make my ideas readable, and to my husband, Michael Ochs, whose editorial experience I drew on as always.

Introduction

Our early years are filled with excitement as we become familiar with the people and the world around us. We awaken each morning anticipating the adventure we face merely by being alive. As we grow older, we assume more and more responsibilities and become aware of imperfections in the universe. In the course of our lives we can become estranged from our initial sense of excitement, exuberance, adventure. We learn that the process of living can actually deaden us, and we want to know how to live so that we can once again feel alive. We recognize this deadness because the world ceases to speak to us. Although the world is no less wonderful, we no longer see it that way, whether in our personal relationships and commitments, our work, or our environment.

Spiritual guidance is first of all about spirituality. Spirituality, as I define it, is "coming into relationship with reality." In spiritual guidance I explicitly name that reality God. Spiritual guidance aims to help clarify and foster the guidee's relationship with God. The field that most nearly resembles spiritual guidance is marriage counseling, in that both practices try to recognize and eliminate any obstacles to the healthy, fruitful, deepening of a relationship.

Spiritual guidance has often been confused with psychotherapy and individual pastoral counseling because the subject matter is so intimate, the discussion is one-on-one, and the problems addressed and the quest for wholeness and healing are similar. But the three techniques can be distinguished from one another in terms of the qualifications of the counselor or guide, the specific problem addressed, the role of God-language, and most important, the ultimate objective of the encounter.

The psychotherapist has years of academic training and usually has to meet licensing standards set by the state. The pastoral counselor is a member of the clergy and frequently has training beyond ordination in order to deal with the problems faced by members of the congregation. The spiritual guide does not have to be ordained, and although the guide may have taken courses in spiritual guidance, most denominations recognize that the ability to be an effective spiritual guide results from a gift for doing it rather than from academic training. Just as many people study piano but only those who are gifted musically eventually become pianists, many people may read the major texts in spirituality, but only a few find themselves called on to become spiritual guides. The spiritual guide's gift has nothing to do with cleverness and the ability to make insightful connections. The gift is to "get out of the way," because ultimately the relationship at stake is not that between the guide and the guidee, but between the guidee and God.

My own formal training was in philosophy. I later worked with—apprenticed with—four different spiritual guides over the course of twenty years. I "discovered" I was a spiritual guide when someone came to me for spiritual guidance. I did not advertise, put up a shingle, or in any way signal that I offered spiritual guidance. I had read in books that those who were meant to be spiritual guides would know it when people actually came to them for spiritual guidance, but I had no idea what that meant or how that might happen. I know only that it did happen, and the reality that people came and continue to come persuaded me that this is what I am meant to do.

Both psychotherapy and pastoral counseling address "problems in living," such as substance abuse, marital difficulties, bereavement, unemployment, difficulty in forming relationships. The psychotherapist may choose a short-term therapy that addresses only the problem at hand or may use the immediate situation as an invitation to address larger patterns of dysfunctional living. The pastoral counselor usually restricts therapy to a few meetings before finding the appropriate referral, given the congregant's specific issues. The spiritual guide is open to discussing any question—Should I take this job? Should I have children? What should I do about my marriage?—and seeks to help the guidee recognize that in addition to yielding an immediate answer, the current situation can be used to intensify the guidee's relationship with God. Bad things will continue to happen, but God's ongoing promise in the Torah is, "I will be with you." Problems are real, but so is the possibility of experiencing life as a journey, with God as companion all along the way.

Psychotherapy has come a long way since Freud critiqued religion as an illusion and his followers typically found "God-talk" to be symptomatic of their patients' unresolved neuroses. Nevertheless, psychotherapy is still not comfortable with religion as the ultimate explanatory principle. For that reason, among others, many people turn for counseling to their clergy rather than the licensed therapy establishment. The pastoral counselor speaks the language of the congregant's faith tradition; the spiritual guide helps each guidee speak the language of the guidee's own experience in the world and, especially, in the guidee's relationship with God.

All three—psychotherapist, pastoral counselor, spiritual guide—have as their objective the healing and ultimate wholeness of the people who come to them. But "wholeness" is defined in different ways by the three groups. For the psychotherapist, wholeness is usually thought of as the capacity to function in this world. For the pastoral counselor, this capacity to function is also a dominant theme, but it is accompanied by the values of the faith tradition shared with the guidee. As a spiritual guide, I recognize that many of the people I see would benefit from psychotherapy and have not hesitated to refer them. The only proviso is that the therapist and the spiritual guide must be told about each other, because both courses of action require complete openness and honesty to be effective. Both courses seek to help the guidee grow, but the spiritual guide is centrally concerned with the growth of the guidee's relationship with God.

Spiritual guidance is a one-on-one relationship that addresses deadness by helping people recognize the presence of God in their lives. It encourages guidees to create a personal view of the world around them. It is meant for adults, that is, people who are old enough to be autonomous. It is also a path that should not, I believe, be prescribed for someone else. It must be freely chosen by those who have the genuine option to walk away from it. Beyond that, the question of deadness can be raised at any stage of life. Indeed, the individuals I have seen range in age from eighteen to eighty-six.

My oldest guidee, Dorothy, was able to find aging itself an adventure. Joan, who was my youngest guidee when she started, found that she could experience deadness in her first job right out of graduate school. Deadness did not always include all aspects of my guidees' experience. They could be alive in their work, like Florence, while sensing that their spiritual life was suddenly unreal.

A major cause of deadness is a failure to inhabit our full selves using all our gifts, living lives that follow other people's agendas for us and do not grow out of our own authenticity. My guidee Marion's coming alive occurred after she reclaimed her love of writing, Deena's from finding a role for dance in her rabbinate. And Paul, even on his deathbed, became more fully alive by recognizing the role of beauty in his philosophy.

This book portrays the quest for aliveness through a series of vignettes, describing people I have worked with very closely over a number of years, with the caveat that these cases are composites of real cases, fictionalized to protect confidentiality but accurate in their portrayal of episodes on the spiritual way. The cases do not have beginnings, forward motion, or endings in the traditional sense because this process is not about curing neuroses or, usually, solving problems. A person's relationship with God, like other relationships, is inherently unfinished, ready to respond to a variety of life situations. Each case is a slice out of the larger, ongoing relationship. Some of these people I continue to see, some have moved away, and others have just moved on. All of them, to one degree or other, have found ways of living their commitments so that their personal relationships with God continue to develop.

The principal question I get from guidees of all ages usually comes disguised. The question "How can I live fully and authentically?" is asked in terms of a marriage problem, a career choice, or an issue with a parent. There is a self that is given to us, shaped by our environment, and shaped by our choices. We long to fully inhabit this self and contribute to the world out of the self's uniqueness. When the self can no longer grow, sing, and breathe easily, we feel pain, unease, and a creeping deadness. We may consent to this lack of feeling rather than face the sharp pain of awakening and being called—or called back—into selfhood. That is why one task of the spiritual guide is to help the guidee overcome fear. The guide must foster a safe space for the guidee to recognize what he or she is being called to and what is being recovered. The guidee must be helped to notice and claim aspects of the self abandoned or unrecognized at an earlier juncture. Somewhere along the way, we are all called to life, to wholeness, to fruitfulness, to joy, and we must sometimes be guided to recognize the call.

The way of spiritual guidance may appear uncharted, and yet certain fundamental assumptions underlie the whole process, as they do in psychotherapy, pastoral counseling, and related pursuits. Behind psychotherapy, for example, lie certain assumptions about human nature, free will, causality, and the like. Underlying spiritual guidance are assumptions that form a very practical theology, one that can be applied to most situations in our lives. The main tenet in this theology is that we are created in the image of God. And as God is one and whole, people, in God's image, aspire to wholeness. When we are in emotional pain, we look for immediate relief in medications, distractions, or the hard work of psychotherapy. But the pain can and should also be regarded as an invitation to strengthen our relationship with God, because the essential unease in our lives finally boils down to the questions of who we are and how we fit into the system as a whole. When we can begin to answer these questions, we can begin to get on with our lives with energy and engagement.

As a Jewish spiritual guide, my methods rely on four gifts we have all received that are as basic to the Jewish worldview as the Exodus and the wandering narrative: story, God, Creation, and being in the image of God.

The Gift of Story

Underlying our choices and actions is a basic story we tell ourselves. Usually we don't tell the whole narrative, only the part of it that relates to a present concern, but implicit in that story is our theology, the fundamental way we structure our experiences. We are always in a story—we have to make sense of all our actions, and narrative form allows us to do so. How we see ourselves can make all the difference, like that between an unwanted child and "the stone the builders rejected [that] has become the chief cornerstone" (Psalm 118:22). Judaism's fundamental gift to us is our people's story, as told in the Torah.

God

Like all good stories, the story in the Torah starts at the beginning. And the first component of that beginning is God. What can we say about God, doubtless the most difficult and least accessible aspect of our story? God is the end of all our journeying, not the beginning. We are tempted to start, as the French philosopher Descartes did, with ourselves, because we at least have access to ourselves, through introspection. But if we start with ourselves, we become by default the center of the universe. Built into a story that started with us would be the radical loneliness of being the sole center of meaning in the universe. So knowing what we don't know and knowing what we can't know, we begin, as Spinoza did, with God. We can do so because God is not a character in the story but the context of the story, and we can focus on the ways in which our own story tells us about more than ourselves.

Creation

The first act in the story is Creation, the subject of a raging, centuries-long debate that has pitted cosmologists, evolutionists, and astronomers favoring the "big bang" theory against proponents of "creation theory" and fundamentalists who interpret the Bible literally. But this debate fails to recognize that the assertion "God created . . ." is not a scientific theory to rival evolution. It frames the basic questions for which we turn to religion: What is our source? Were we an accident, or were we planned for and wanted? And once we are here, how are we judged? When we introspect and examine the questions that really concern us, they are not about how a lifeless planet turned into one teeming with life of all degrees of complexity. We are basically self-centered, yearning to know if we were wanted, and the Bible answers that question in the crucial word "created." And in case we are slow to understand, the Bible spells out the creative process repeatedly, showing how the world is created, how relationships are created, and how a people is created, thereby reminding us that we ourselves are creators and that creativity is a sacred activity. Beginning with God's pronouncement in Genesis that the Creation was good, we can go on to see the connection of Creation to our own process of contributing to the universe.

Being in the Image of God

When the Torah describes our own creation, the aspect of the story that most concerns us, it adds the crucial statement that we were created in the image of God. We may feel that in some aspects we are a failed creation, but this gift can bring us immediate feelings of delight, of freedom, of being at home in the world. God is creator, so we are creators; God remembers, so we remember; God makes a covenant with us, so we enter into covenant; God cares, so we learn to be caring. The realization that we are in the image of God begins to answer the question "What can we hope for?"

As Jews, we believe in the essential goodness of our children and the educational philosophy that flows from that; we highly value relationships modeled on our relationship with God; and we believe in genuine standards: some things are true and some are not. These principles engage us ever more deeply in a world that is real and is lovingly shaped, one in which we can be at home. These positions differ profoundly from the Christian view that has favored isolating oneself from the world and undertaking unnatural, ascetic practices, and from the view that "through Adam's fall we sinnéd all," as a nineteenth-century reader for children stated. They are also at odds with the fundamental assumptions of existential psychoanalysis, which identifies four human problems, foremost among them the fact and awareness that we die, and secondarily the burden of being free. Both of these are considered part of the third problem, the larger reality that life is meaningless. The fourth problem for existentialists is that we are alone.

As a spiritual guide committed to the values of Judaism, I challenge every one of those points. Death need not be the end of the story. As my guidee David discovered, there is only this universe, so we cannot fall out of it. The Jewish view of essential trust in God's goodness and in the meaningfulness of Creation sees death as part of this purposeful system, not as the final answer. Freedom is indeed a burden, creating vertigo and nausea, but only when there are no structures to guide us. Indeed, freedom can be experienced as the greatest gift, and when it grows out of knowing who we are, it feels like liberation. The essential Jewish view is that there *is* meaning in life—not merely the meanings we create, but also the meanings we discover. Finally, to the argument that we are irreversibly alone, Judaism counters with the repeated promise from God throughout the *Tanach*: "I will be with you." Not only are we not, finally, alone, but at the heart of Judaism we find the primacy of relationship. We did not create ourselves, and we are not our own ends.

Judaism's commitments can be stated as follows:

1. *God is one.*
The central concept of *the One* as a simple, whole, and complete explanatory system lies behind our attempts at unifying ourselves, an important goal of spiritual guidance.

2. *We were created . . .*
Because we were created, we assume a Creator and a plan, and therefore it makes sense for us to look for meaning. Meaning is discovered, not created. We can assume a first cause (the Maker or Doer) and also a final cause (the purpose or good of something).

3. *. . . in the image of God.*

Our essential nature makes us a significant part of Creation. While this divine aspect is already true of us, it needs to be recognized and claimed. Jewish spiritual guides approach all of our guidees with an awareness of their inherent worth and a sense of the holiness that infuses our encounter.

4. *We were enslaved . . .*

The Exodus story is not merely a past historical event; it says something about our personal situation and becomes the formative way of thinking about our current condition.

5. *. . . but we were liberated . . .*

Liberation and freedom of the individual from whatever binds us are essential goals in Jewish spiritual guidance.

6. *. . . and given revelation.*

Freedom occurs within structures that help us actualize our essential nature of being in the image of God. Revelation was, and revelation is— and part of our task is to recognize the revelations within our own lives.

7. *We entered into covenant.*

Learning to make promises that will transform us through our efforts to live up to them is the essential way we grow in our effort to be in God's image.

8. *We wandered for forty years in the wilderness . . .*

Revelation is not a truth that can be told but a truth that must be realized over time in each of our lives.

9. *. . . and we entered the Promised Land.*

The Torah ends with Moses not living to see the Israelites enter the Promised Land. Spiritual guides, as well, see successive approaches to each person's wholeness but are not privileged to actually see anyone entering into full selfhood.

These essential Jewish landmarks are never far from my consciousness as I listen to people's stories and try to help them discern their relationships with God. And this book is a tribute to the people who have claimed themselves and so found joy on the spiritual way.

I

DEENA

Bringing a Love of Dance into Worship

Deena started taking dance lessons when she was five and continued to dance in musicals and shows throughout her high school and college years. She was slim and carried herself with that unmistakable poise and grace that dancers seem to be born with. Her dark brown hair was usually tied in a bun, but when she let it out, it reached below her waist. After college, thinking she "needed time to decide what I wanted to be when I grew up," she had taken a job with a Jewish children's social agency. Even so, she found time to continue dancing, although much less than before.

Of the people she met at the agency, one impressed her especially. Jacob Rosenthal, a Conservative rabbi, seemed to have a magic touch with children. They flocked around him constantly, and when she visited his synagogue one Shabbat, she saw that he was equally popular with congregants of all ages. She got to know him quite well during her first year of work, and following a remark he made that she would make a great rabbi, she decided to explore the clergy as a career option. By the middle of her second year at the agency, she had been accepted to the rabbinical program at the Reform seminary where I teach.

At first glance, Deena's case may read more like one of vocational, rather than spiritual, guidance. But narrowing our focus doesn't get us nearer to God. Rather, we must open ourselves to an ever-wider vision of reality. Unfortunately, many people believe that life demands they abandon earlier passions as they move on to their professional development. Later, they come to regret the "road not taken" and dream of retirement, when they can retrace some of those steps. But service to God demands that we bring all of ourselves into play. We will see that when Deena reclaimed dance, she also opened herself to new friendships and a better relationship with her senior rabbi. These are not *in addition* to a deepening relationship with God; they *are* the deepening relationship. As I listen for the subtle motion of God's urgings in my guidee's life, I listen with the awareness that the spiritual life is the most capacious life possible.

I first met Deena when she was starting the third year of training for the rabbinate. She found her way to my office, which is situated in a cul-de-sac off the first floor at the seminary. I have been offered a more accessible office but decided that the room I had provided maximum privacy for my guidees. To maintain confidentiality, I ask each guidee to agree to two ground rules. "The first," I say, "is that anything said here between us stays in this room." I emphasize the last four words, as much to assure them of confidentiality as to express my own wish that they not quote—or rather, misquote—me to someone else. "The second is that *you* set the agenda. This is your time; use it as you please."

Deena came to me for spiritual guidance because of a specific problem she had had with boundaries while interning at Temple Beth Hakodesh for the summer. Many congregants use their temple community as a place to play out the dynamics of their home situations. They love the congregation and, at the same time, act as the "rebellious child"; for example, they make a habit of criticizing the rabbi but need the rabbi to be the "grown-up" in their lives. Deena had become friends with two women in the congregation who were about her age. She met them regularly for coffee but once dropped her guard and started joining in their discussions about other members of the temple. She stopped meeting them so informally after that, realizing that she was not playing her proper role. Although no apparent harm had come of her indiscretion, the incident disturbed her enough to ask me for advice, and she continued to see me monthly after that about other matters that bothered her.

Over the next few months, Deena talked about an issue she had both with following authority and exercising it. The problem, it turned out, was part of an ongoing internal battle for liberation (her term). She had begun her struggle for freedom long before I met her, in dealing with her parents' disappointment at having a girl and with the restricted role in life they expected her to play. That she was an ardent feminist was shocking enough to her traditional immigrant parents, Jews from the Ukraine, but it was nothing like their surprise when she chose to study for the rabbinate. To their credit, they had actually come to take pride in her achievements.

She said that she wanted to grow in all the ways she could during her short time in seminary. (She was, and still is, the only seminarian who used the word "short" in describing the five-year course of study.) She wondered how she could know, at the age of twenty-six, which gifts she should bring to God and which would have to be left behind. She was giving up dancing seriously because she didn't want to take time away from her studies. Besides, she said, she was no longer as physically fit as she had been earlier. (Was this a rationalization? We should all be as physically fit as she looked to me.) She would be continuing her internship at Beth Hakodesh during her third year of seminary. The skills she had learned while working at the agency, she said, were already serving her well in meeting with congregants and helping them sort though their many concerns. She took the name of the temple, which translates as "House of the Holy," very earnestly: "Where better to do God's work?" she said.

One of the first initiatives Deena took at Beth Hakodesh was to set up a story time for the very young, which she held in a separate room during the Friday night service. She then expanded this popular activity to Sabbath morning "Tot Shabbat" services for two- to four-year-olds. Her internship was the most successful Beth Hakodesh had ever had, and Rabbi Fromm had told her that she would be most welcome there as assistant rabbi after she was ordained, if the congregation were large enough by then to afford hiring one. It wasn't. She did, however, get a sparkling letter of recommendation from Rabbi Fromm, and she was quickly snapped up as assistant rabbi by Stanley Gold, of Temple Ohav Shalom in Brooklyn.

She was in her second year at Ohav Shalom—"Something always seems to happen to me in my second year, wherever I am"—when she came to see me on a Monday, her official day off. It had been more than a year since our last meeting, the High Holy Days were over with, the trees in Washington Square Park were losing their leaves, and I was deep into fall semester classes. When I asked her how things were going, she said that she and Rabbi Gold were getting along beautifully and the congregants have taken her to heart. By all objective measures, everything was great. "But," she said,

> I keep having to tell myself that I'm blessed, fulfilled, and content. I have to tell myself these things, because I don't believe them and want to convince myself. Is it possible that I wasn't meant to be a rabbi?

I asked her to bring me up to date on her doings since I'd last seen her, which was shortly after she had begun at Ohav Shalom. She sighed, and began by repeating that everyone at the temple was being really wonderful to her and that the board, the president, and Rabbi Gold couldn't be more warm and encouraging. She then said that she had had some trouble taking on the professionalism required by her role. As she described it:

> I still wanted to be the excited, happy congregant who breaks rules and flouts authority, only now I was in charge. As you know, my problem with a couple of congregants during my first year as intern taught me that while authority may be a burden, my congregants need me to play the role of "grown-up."

The previous winter, on what felt like a whim (although later she could say it was God's gift), she had begun attending dance classes for

the first time in years. The timing seemed right, she said—a long time
had passed since her last serious dancing—and the location was con-
venient. She felt guilty about the classes, which met three times a
week, and didn't want anyone in the congregation to know what she
was doing. How, I asked, could she take off so much time without
anyone noticing? "My congregants think I'm in therapy—most of
them are (well, maybe not most, but lots)—so they tread gingerly
around the subject of my absences." Although she joked about it, she
kept her penciled-in hours for class inviolable, except for deaths and
other emergencies.

   In her dance classes, Deena found that she could become completely absorbed in her body once again and praise God the way she
used to: by flexing a muscle, arching a limb. She took a liturgical
dance workshop and a dance midrash class, where students acted out
biblical stories in a way that allowed them to find meanings beyond
those explicit in the text. To make up for the hours she missed, she
held frequent evening meetings and breakfast study groups. These
were well attended, and the rabbinic work seemed to be going well.
And she had now started to incorporate dance—she called it movement—into her services.

   It began with a special healing service last spring that a few congregants had requested. I'd heard about healing services, but I'd
   never attended one, much less run one. I had no idea what typical healing services were like, so I asked around and got all different answers. I learned that they were usually homegrown
   services and that they attracted people for all different reasons.
   That was certainly true at mine: one congregant had had uter-
   ine cancer followed by a hysterectomy and was now undergoing
   chemotherapy. Another was trying to weather a painful divorce.
   And, as you've seen in the papers, there was that vicious anti-
   Semitic graffiti at our temple following the flare-up in Brooklyn
   between Jews and African-Americans. Our members were
   extremely shaken up by that, so I tried to organize a communal
   service that would include people from various synagogues and

black churches. I met some wonderful clergy in the neighborhood—ministers, priests, an imam—and everybody thought it was a great idea. But after going back to our congregations and sounding out some of our members, we all concluded that the time wasn't ripe yet for such intermingling, although we promised to keep in touch and to keep each other in mind.

So I picked out prayers and meditations for our own service and then decided that I wanted to include some movement as well. Nine people showed up at the service, all female. I offered participants a chance to speak about the healing they sought. It took some time before the woman with cancer began talking about her need for some way to find healing or, at least, comfort. That opened the floodgates.

I had the participants stand up and started some quiet music. I'd carefully chosen pieces to which people could move without too much effort. I began with "Spring" from Vivaldi's *Four Seasons* and continued with works that were less and less familiar—I wanted them to get involved with their movement, not with the music.

One teenager said she'd long been praying for a miracle cure for acne. A woman who was nudging seventy said she would be happy to wake up just one morning free of the arthritis that prevented her from enjoying life. Little by little, as the world outside the room was falling away, people began to move—an arm, a hip, a head. Gradually, they were moving their whole bodies, unself-consciously (never mind what the other members of the congregation might think). At last, through movement, they could express their fear, their anguish, their hopes. The service was a great success, and several of the people who were there asked when the next one would be.

All the while, though, I was going through my own personal crisis. A phrase from the musical *A Chorus Line* kept running through my mind over the music I was playing for the service: "God, I'm a dancer; a dancer dances." So if I'm a dancer, I should live out my most authentic self and give up being a rabbi.

After the first healing service, Deena thought she might hold another, on Shavuot, seven weeks after Passover. Because the festival marked the Jews' receiving the Torah at Mount Sinai, it seemed to her a perfect occasion to celebrate with dance. Although Shavuot (also known as Pentecost, or the Feast of Weeks) is technically as important a holiday as Passover, attendance at temple services is usually sparse. "And anyhow," she explained,

> summer is a less formal time for many synagogues. I simply posted a notice of a dance/healing body workshop open to all. I hoped to lure a few men, so I wrote on the notice that "everyone is welcome, and I mean everyone." Thirty people came to that second meeting, including a few who were not members of the congregation, and three men, all of whom had been brought by women who came.
>
> Even with that spectacular growth, I was not prepared for the third workshop: ninety people showed up! The original nine continued, and I recognized many from the second workshop, but the new group included a contingent from a black Baptist congregation, as well as residents of a nearby nursing home. I had to open up the day school's gym to accommodate the crowd. And since one teacher for a group of ninety wouldn't do, I deputized people from the first workshop, so the large group could break up into circles of eight or nine.
>
> I began, as I always did, with prayer and with a brief sharing of stories about our bodies. As the participants slowly began moving, while trying to heal wounds of abuse, sickness, and neglect, I was awed by one of the Baptists, a large woman in her late forties who must have weighed close to 250 pounds. Although one leg was obviously deformed, she danced! And she cried.
>
> It was Agnes, the minister of the Baptist church, whom I'd met at the interfaith meeting we'd had after the riots. She confessed to having loaded up the church bus and driven a group of her congregants to the workshop after seeing a notice on the supermarket bulletin board.

Two weeks later, I visited Agnes's church and found the service electrifying. The building, a wooden structure dating from the early 1900s, was outfitted with wooden benches, a simple pulpit, and not much else. The windows along the side were colorfully painted with angular designs, and a large bronze cross hung on the front wall. Before it, on risers, stood a gospel choir of at least sixty girls, boys, men, and women, all dressed in blue robes with yellow trim. I say stood, but they really never stopped moving during the entire service. They rocked from side to side, clapped their hands, snapped their fingers, raised their arms high over their heads with fingers shaking, all the while singing exuberantly or humming, even during parts of the sermon. There must have been 150 congregants, and every one of them was completely engaged, feeling free to call out "amen," "tell us, sister," "praise the Lord," and similar phrases. It was impossible to be in the church during the service and not get caught up in the excitement. I was struck that here it was, an ordinary Sunday, and the people were obviously profoundly moved by the service.

Agnes attended the next Shabbat service at our temple. Seeing it through her eyes, I felt embarrassed about our worship, because it wasn't nearly as involving for the congregants as her Baptist service seemed to be. But Agnes really liked it and found much in it to praise. She loved the way the congregants kissed the Torah as it was being marched around the Temple. "Your people sure love that Torah," she said. Agnes also liked the Torah chanting but found the rest of the music not to her taste. "And they're too passive, just sitting there. You've got to get them up! Move them in their bodies as well as in their heads." I knew I could learn a lot from Agnes, although I didn't want to turn Ohav Shalom into a Baptist church.

After the relative success of the three summer workshops, Deena felt ready to include movement in a regular service, not a special healing service. Although she herself had a dancer's body, she felt strongly that all bodies were meant to dance. She frequently spoke to her congregation about the importance of the body, explaining how Judaism's refusal to separate mind from body was one of its great strengths. For example, Judaism does not say that only the soul is immortal and that the soul is therefore more important than the body. On the contrary, in the world-to-come, the entire being will be alive again. For that reason, deliberate and permanent disfigurement of the body is forbidden; among the Orthodox, tattoos are forbidden. Deena continued what had turned into a monologue:

> A healing service/workshop, which people specifically and deliberately attended, was one thing—it had certainly tapped into a lot of goodwill in the congregation. But inflicting my weird views about movement on folks attending a regular service was something else entirely. Any introduction of body movement during the service would have to be very carefully structured and choreographed. Most important, it needed the support of Rabbi Gold, who was something of a traditionalist.
>
> To my surprise, he was very open to my idea and suggested that I take over part of the service for Rosh HaShanah morning. He thought that immediately following his sermon would be perfect, "when people will have been sitting for a long time dozing off," he said. To think that I would be leading movement prayer during the High Holy Day services! But what would I do? I kept ruminating—talking to Agnes, to Rabbi Gold (he agreed to my introducing movement but deliberately left all the planning to me), and to a few of the congregants who had liked the healing services so much. Some of my congregants are real live wires.

Deena reported happily that the congregation didn't see the change as revolutionary and thought it had fit in almost seamlessly. And, "wonder of wonders," she said, about a dozen men had actually gotten up to dance. She was now busily planning for Simchat Torah, when the annual cycle of Torah reading ends with the final chapter, describing Moses's death, and is immediately begun again with the opening chapter of Genesis. The service for the holiday already included movement: marching with the Torahs around the temple and dancing that often spilled out into the street. She had purchased tambourines, finger cymbals, and small, egg-shaped maracas, so that every Torah in the procession would be accompanied by singing and dancing. Again, the congregation took her ideas in good spirit, although when she thought about the Baptist church service, she thought they—and she—still had a long way to go.

She then tried to sum up what she had accomplished and learned.

> It's amazing to discover that what I've always taught others is true even when applied to myself. I've encouraged so many others to claim their gifts and suggested that using their talents fully is one of the greatest services they can do for the world. And now, by reclaiming my dancing, I've added to my rabbinate, inspired members of my congregation, and made each day at work joyful and exhilarating. And in Agnes I've found a colleague and a friend—we will have many more exchanges between her church and our temple. I guess I've been given a gift of community just because I wanted to share what dance has given me.

I told her that she had come to see me with a question and asked her if she remembered what it was. She said she wasn't sure and asked to be reminded. "You were wondering," I said, "if you should give up the rabbinate and concentrate on dancing or vice versa. But in telling me all about what you've been doing, it seems to me that you've answered your own question. You've seamlessly (your word) integrated dance into your rabbinical duties, and both you and the congregation have benefited. As far as I can see, you don't need to give up either of the pursuits you love."

Then, as a coup de grace, I delivered my "no pain, no gain" theory of religion, pointing out that somewhere she had gotten the notion that she could not be a good rabbi unless she gave up something else that she cared about deeply. One's authentic self, or essence, is not embodied in a single-minded pursuit of any one thing. I wanted her to see and, above all, to *feel* that her interest in dance brought her to a fuller life, allowing her to make use of *all* her gifts in the service of others.

2

DOROTHY
Dealing with Aging

It was a special privilege to work with Dorothy; bright and outspoken, she had humor, warmth, and a perspective shaped out of her own wisdom and the gift of age.

Dorothy was a sprightly seventy-four-year-old widow whose husband had died of a heart attack nearly twenty-five years earlier. She had one son, Sammy, now in his early forties, and three grandchildren. She took some time to describe her son, for whom she made more excuses than I thought necessary. Where Dorothy was feisty and assertive, Sammy was timid. Where she cared passionately about a whole range of issues, he was content to accept the world as it presented itself. After college, he had taken a clerical job with an insurance company in Boston but, since being promoted to actuary a few years later, had not taken any steps to improve himself or his position. He thought of his work as a job, not a career, a stance that Dorothy found hard to accept.

Dorothy spoke of her son and his wife, Joan, with a tinge of disappointment and sadness, but her eyes sparkled when she discussed her three grandchildren, all under ten. Her unconditional love for them was embodied in her standing offer to babysit whenever and wherever, no questions asked. When she was not speaking of her "little ones," as she called them, Dorothy maintained a refreshing reserve, as well as manners that have gone out of style these days. She kept her voice modulated, never interrupted, and shunned any untoward language.

Dorothy had been retired for six years after a busy career, first as a jazz vocalist (she had once opened for Benny Goodman's Orchestra, she told me proudly) and later as a registered nurse. Astonished as I was by this unusual combination of activities, Dorothy would surprise me with much more before we were done. She first wrote to me in response to an article of mine about the spiritual life that had been reproduced in her synagogue's newsletter. We had been corresponding for a few months when she asked whether we might work together on spiritual guidance. After all these years, I found the formulation "work together on spiritual guidance" an inspired choice of words. It was never clear who was guiding whom— we both found growth through our interaction.

Our initial face-to-face meeting took place in my office. From our phone conversations, I had pictured a tall, forceful-looking woman with a bone-crushing handshake. In fact she was short and slight, except for a little bulge around her middle. She shook hands firmly and confidently. A few wisps of gray hair had managed to escape the last combing she had applied to her short, neatly trimmed cut. Her most striking feature, though, was a pair of sky-blue eyes that could, I imagined, penetrate my head and read my thoughts. Their color was accented even more by the blue suits that she liked to wear. I was hardly settled in my chair when she began, cryptically: "Aging is night and the desert all over again."

Dorothy, as I would soon discover, often thought at length before talking and then spoke in shorthand. Here she was invoking the Dark Night of the Soul, the fourth of five stages on the spiritual way— described a century ago by Evelyn Underhill—that have since been adopted in some form or other by most writers on spirituality. The Dark Night is a time of trial, purgation, and tempering that precedes the final stage, Union, when we are transformed from the self we have been to the self we are meant to become. The desert, in her statement, was shorthand for the Israelites' forty years of wandering in the wilderness following their exodus from Egypt. She saw the time in the desert as being the Israelites' Dark Night of the Soul, which prepared them for reaching the Promised Land. She continued:

> You finally have to lay to rest the ghosts of your past and face up to your mortality. In that sense, aging is a natural route to enlightenment, and you can "jump ahead" with a concerted spiritual effort. But even aging doesn't do the job automatically— just look at all the old people who live in denial and have never dealt with their own vulnerability. When I say "concerted spiritual effort" I mean staying open, aware, and awake, and keeping your defenses down. You can't do it by willpower—you have to release control and really taste your own vulnerability.

Dorothy was very consciously moving into old age. She was fighting osteoporosis, an arthritic knee that restricted her walking, and mild digestive problems—she could no longer eat some of her favorite foods without "paying a price," as she put it. Her most serious problem, though, was macular degeneration in both of those beautiful eyes, making it progressively harder to read. "First, they blamed my impending blindness on smoking, which I gave up more than ten years ago. Don't say it!" she said, holding up her hand.

> As a nurse, I knew better, but I funneled all my potential vices into this one, which I considered more of an indiscretion than the criminal act it seems to be now. Anyway, according to the latest reports, there's no connection between smoking and macular degeneration. Next year they'll probably decide that smoking is good for you. But I digress. My theory about the tasks we face at different stages of life is that as infants, all we can do is digest; as old people we can determine our relationship to the world—how to construe what is happening.

I asked if she would elaborate on her somewhat puzzling remark. She was, she said, giving me the punch line of a long train of thought.

Old age is often characterized as a return to childhood. Just as a child cannot support itself, feed itself, even care for its most basic bodily functions, so the old person slips gradually into a stage of not being able to perform these tasks. But there are monumental differences. As infants, we have to take in everything—what we see, what we hear, what we eat—and somehow assimilate it. When we are old, we already have a value system that shapes all our perceptions, so while the infant and the old person look as if they are doing the same thing, the infant passively takes in experiences, while the old person actively helps shape them.

This brief elaboration explained a lot of what I saw in Dorothy. She was, in fact, restricted in what she could do, but I had rarely met someone who exuded such energy. With her brief thought experiment about the aged person and the infant, she proved to herself that she could actively change the way she perceived and construed her world. I tried to understand how Dorothy's nursing fit in with her jazz singing and her spirituality. She explained:

Improvisation for the jazz musician comes about from such thorough immersion in both the music and the technique that the performer no longer has to think about them and can make them the servants of the vision. Similarly, when the self is mastered as completely as the technique of music, the self can be in the service of a vision—in my case, making the world a little bit better by alleviating pain and helping others cure themselves— instead of the vision having to prop up a self.

When I allowed yet again that her insights were taking too cryptic a form, she laughed, as she did regularly and heartily, and offered a series of examples where the self is used but not focused on. She mentioned some fearsome instances of the single-mindedness that comes to a nurse in the midst of a medical emergency, but her preferred examples all involved play. Play, she felt, meant going beyond the necessities of simple survival, and that was where spirituality could be expressed and discovered. So her jazz singing was an example of self-forgetfulness, much like her earlier field hockey playing. I strained to picture this woman as an avid field hockey player, but then I remembered endless afternoons my friends and I spent running back and forth in the park near my house trying to beat the other team in tag and being completely oblivious to time, place, and even the world immediately around us.

Dorothy continued by saying that we cannot possibly gain wisdom until we have lived through certain experiences, which is why wisdom is the unique gift of older people. She thought that gaining it may well be enough to make old age worth the inconveniences and allow us to avoid looking back with longing to our youth.

> I don't find myself thinking back to earlier times with nostalgia or longing. I feel my whole life has been a progressive move toward freedom, so I'm grateful not to be my younger self. What I love about being old is that I don't have to depend on other people's opinions anymore—I find greater satisfaction using my own judgment. I had to learn to be patient with the time that this reorientation took.

Time, I allowed, or, rather, our relationship to time, is one of the ways we create meaning.

> Yes, and when we recognize that to everything there is a season, we get to the heart of our relationship with time. For example, I've observed the aging process in my own body since childhood, when relatives invariably greeted me with "My, how you've grown." Then, during adolescence, my body became a foreign country to explore. We only realize our body's full potential in union with another's—and some of us become carriers of new life. In parenting we see how amazing our bodies are as we relive, through our children, the wonder of our own personal discovery. Years pass, and the rapid transformations

that we went through during the first part of life slow down so much that we're tempted to think of our bodies as more stable than they really are. But then, a series of physical changes makes us see our bodies in a radically new way. No longer are height or weight or strength or fatigue so important, but the smaller motions we didn't notice before now claim our attention.

I used to leap from my bed in the morning. Now, as it takes me longer to gather my strength, I notice what returning consciousness means in every aspect of my body. I marvel at the body's wisdom—it's been telling me things all along, but there was always so much to do that I couldn't afford to notice. My visceral reactions tell me who I like and who I don't. My body clearly tells me when I'm really unhappy, even when my friends exclaim how happy I must be. Sometimes the body speaks through the loud trumpet of illness and breakdown. More often it speaks through the quieter voice of little aches, or fatigue, or a burst of energy, or a sense of physical well-being.

In the past I was proud of my ability to ignore bodily clues. I reveled in my stoicism and didn't let little things get me down. I had an arsenal of Band-Aids, aspirin, and antacids to see me through, and I kept moving past every welcoming resting place.

How would my life have looked if I'd taken my body's wisdom seriously twenty years earlier? What if I'd realized that my headaches were subtle indications of a growing enslavement to other people's standards and expectations? I was already a full-time nurse and a full-time mother, but I felt obliged to bake cookies instead of just buying some for the PTA meeting. I was pushing myself to justify my having a career when it was far less common for women to work than it is now. Since then, I'm happy to say, I've realized that having a little dust on the piano lid doesn't make me a bad person. Even so, I can't look back without regretting all the times I blocked my body's wisdom from reaching and affecting me. But the call hasn't stopped. If I've been wrong, I can still be right. I can explore how aging can yet be an adventure and a glorious fruition.

Dorothy felt a growing sense of freedom as she let go of artificial, external standards such as cooking, baking, and cleaning house. At the same time, however, growing older was accompanied by a growing sense of loss: her friends were dying off at a rapid pace. She had become an inveterate reader of the obituary page. It was the first thing she opened to in the *New York Times*, and in any given week, she was likely to find the names of one or two people she had known. During one particularly harrowing week, she learned of five such deaths. The people were not all close—several she had not been in touch with for years—but clearly, the ranks of her contemporaries were thinning out. I marveled that she could go on with such joy and energy. She added:

> In seasons of mourning we can deepen our love. I believe that through mourning we're meant to learn more than just endurance and stoicism. We can learn how to love something that's beyond our grasp but still in our heart and memory.

I told her of my belief that growing older is a process of stripping away the attachments and loves that have distracted us from the love of God. I like the concept of de-selfing. We could focus her interest in the story of Exodus on the misery and suffering of the Israelites in Egypt and on the horrible plagues that preceded their departure. Similarly, we could focus on the many losses that aging brings us: of people we love, of meaningful work, of the health and strength we used to enjoy. But we could also look at the Israelites' story as a move toward some desirable goals, such as freedom and an intimacy with God. In the same way, we can reinterpret our aging as a move toward a sense of self, independent of all the roles we have played.

We get de-selfed through all the tempering we experience in our lives: our children grow up, our parents die, our friends drift away, our eyes grow dim—as Dorothy knew better than most—and our strength dissipates. But de-selfing isn't just negative; we de-self because we're pursuing love, and contemplating this idea can speed the process.

Shortly before Passover, Dorothy appeared with an air of mischie-
vousness I hadn't seen before. She told me she was adding her own
commentary to the Passover Haggadah: aging as one interpretation of
the plagues visited by God on the Egyptians, who were keeping the
Israelites in slavery.

> The first plague is the transformation of water into blood. My
> interpretation is that the first relatively minor—but very real—
> step in aging is the reversal of our usual sources of nourishment.

When I expressed bewilderment, she laughed and explained that
this idea was what actually triggered her whole reinterpretation of
the plagues. She had attended a meeting held at her old college, and
for lunch they had all repaired to the college cafeteria. "How in the
world do they eat those things?" she remarked, describing the greasy
pizza, the hamburgers, the french fries—obviously not a cafeteria for
people of her age. The "clear water" she used to drink there had
turned to blood.

> The second plague is an infestation of frogs, a symbol of fertil-
> ity. But when we age, we are no longer fertile.
>   The third plague, of gnats or lice, represents the pesky but
> not yet dangerous illnesses of aging.
>   The fourth plague also consists of insects, in the form of flies,
> but now a distinction is drawn between the masters and the
> slaves: this plague affected all of Egypt except Goshen, where
> the Israelites lived.

Dorothy's interpretation was that for those who are not spiritually
involved—the Egyptians, in this case—there is no real distinction
between plagues three and four. But for the Israelites, who have
begun to get a spiritual perspective, the fourth plague allows them to
draw a distinction between aging as a pesky situation and aging as a
religious wake-up call.

The fifth plague is cattle disease, which is related to retirement. Cattle served as a major source of livelihood, and the disease took that away, just as retirement means loss of livelihood. I do get a small pension, but inflation is eating away its value.

The sixth plague is boils. I believe that illness functions as a wake-up call for all older people, whether they are spiritual or not. Job, for example, was unmoved by all his losses, so (the biblical text tells us) Satan got permission to attack his body and inflicted boils from the soles of his feet to the crown of his head.

"This is my 'boils theory of spirituality,'" Dorothy quipped, "not my route at all."

The seventh plague, hail, and the eighth, locusts, destroy all the crops and bring us to the heart of aging: we are no longer productive and we are cut off from future productivity.

The ninth plague is darkness, and I won't even talk about my macular degeneration. But I will talk about the metaphoric darkness that grows as we age. In childhood everything is dark, mysterious, unknown, and beyond control. Between forty and fifty we reach the midday of life, when all is brightly illuminated: we feel competent at what we do, and we believe we can understand anything if we put our minds to it. But as we age, we recognize how little we ever knew and how very little was really under our control. Aging brings us back to darkness.

And the tenth plague, of course, is death.

Despite her play on the plagues, Dorothy was remarkably cheerful about aging.

Time doesn't have to be our master, it can be our friend. I've seen that woundedness and vulnerabilities are challenges through which we make our contribution. A friend I met on my first nursing job, a lovely woman who worked on the children's cancer ward, had a noticeable speech defect. She was extremely shy, which suggested to me that she'd been teased as a young-ster. But if that was so, the same teasing also gave her great empathy and tenderness for the children in her care. She was wonderful at making them feel comfortable with themselves despite their loss of hair, distended abdomens, and constant exhaustion.

So, not being impervious to time is, in fact, one of our gifts. People talk about wanting to be young again. I don't want to be young again—I've been there, done that! I'm at a different point in life, and although I have declining energy, I also believe I've experienced genuine gains. I've been "tempered by time" and by the insights into the experiences that I gained over time. I no longer want my sense of worth to be external. I no longer want to believe that miracles come in the form of letters or phone calls that will change my life. The changes I value come from my relationship to God and to my self. The plague of darkness is crucial, because we really have to enter into unknowing in order to be transformed. As long as we hold onto the belief that we know, then we cannot change. Change is real, and I not only accept it, I welcome it. "To everything there is a season."

We have all met people for whom aging is a fitting culmination of their lives. They stand as witnesses to what a life lived in deepening relationship with God might look like. They shine with age's new happiness: at last they have transcended guilt and self-hatred. They live fully in the present and have even come to accept their mortal-ity. Their pain and grief are as real as they are for all of us, but they see life in perspective and don't withdraw because they suffer. They trust that however great the pain, the joy is deeper still.

Over the next few months, Dorothy and I began to elaborate on another of her pet theories: covenant as being our relationship to time. Together we identified four covenants that we, as spiritual beings, enter into, and formulated them all as giving shape to time: our covenants with the future, the present, and the past, and our covenant with God, which expresses eternity.

Our covenant with the future, we determined, includes our covenant with the next generation—our own children or those of others. We don't have to be parents to be deeply committed to the next generation. We care about the environment, education, and legislation that will help the world become a better place for those who follow us.

Dorothy then gave a disquisition on parenting drawn largely from her own experience:

> The covenant of parenthood may seem simple, natural, easy, but babies aren't always cute and cuddly. They can keep you up for three nights in a row, they can fuss, and you can feel totally ineffectual as you try to comfort them. And that's the easy part. They turn into adolescents and define themselves by their opposition to you.
>
> When Sammy was a junior in high school, he dropped down a level in English, from college prep to general education. I was furious because, on a whim, I felt he was closing off future options. "I'll be darned if I'm going to write fifteen papers each semester," he said. It was true that his teacher was referred to by the students as "Miss Fifteen," but by going into gen. ed., I believed he would lessen his chances of majoring in a humanities subject in college. Deep down, though, I think I didn't like the idea that he was placing himself with the less gifted students.
>
> Children can leave you wondering what would have happened if you hadn't been mother to this son or daughter: Would your relationship have endured beyond that fight? You would never accept such a rejection of values from a friend who asked for your advice—it would quickly cool your relationship.

And there she identified precisely what distinguishes a covenantal relationship from an acquaintance and even from most friendships.

Continuing on, we agreed that our covenant with the future provides a goal that can carry us forth when we feel mired in some swamp. Such a covenant marked Joseph's true growth in his relationship with God: "So Joseph made the sons of Israel swear, saying, 'When God has taken notice of you, you shall carry up my bones from here'" (Genesis 50:25).

Dorothy and I agreed that our covenant with the present is more easily identified, especially when it is embodied, as it often is, in a life partner, a sibling, or a close friend—one we love uniquely and with full commitment, someone whose presence in our lives feels like a "given." We count on this love to help us deal with unforeseen changes in the people we love and in ourselves. Those we love most are precisely the ones who can hurt us the most. In a covenant, polite behavior does not work: we have to be honest, which means that harsh words are sometimes exchanged. Because we know each other so well, we can say exactly those things that most upset the other person. Very little has the potential to give us more pain—and more joy—than an honest conversation with one we love.

Dorothy's husband, Herbert, had been a pharmacist; they met considerably later than most couples did in those days—after Dorothy had stopped singing professionally and taken up nursing. Herbert was sweet, and she had clearly loved him. Indeed, through him and his love for her, Dorothy found the courage to fight for her place in the world. She had that tendency anyway, she said, but with him she knew she had someone on her side. She even believed that although he was long gone, his support was still helping her "learn to enjoy my life, appreciate my own talents, and revel in my newly found freedom."

Finally, Dorothy and I tackled our covenant with the past, which is embodied in concern for our parents and for the people of their and earlier generations. Many of the virtues we acquire in parenting find new applications as we nurture those who were once our caregivers. For example, Dorothy had had to care for her mother, who was declining but who had outlived Herbert by four years. When Dorothy had to provide comfort and reassurance before her mother's frequent medical tests, she found herself drawing on her experience in cheering up her son, rather than using the similar skills she had developed during her years of nursing: "My bedside manner took on a completely different quality when my mother was the patient."

But even when our covenant with the past is not with specific individuals, it finds expression in our care for tradition, which is the gift of those who came before, and for the world we inherited. Dorothy explained:

> Passover was my most important and enduring tradition. I began running our extended-family seder even before I was married, and it was hard to pass it on to Sammy because he might not run it the same way. But Sammy wanted his own children to grow up with the experience of helping prepare for a seder at their house, and a few years ago I reluctantly agreed to let him do it. The first seder at his house was, in fact, wonderful. I loved seeing the little ones' eyes light up when we enjoyed the *charoset* they had prepared out of ground almonds and sweet grape juice. And they almost jumped out of their seats when we all feigned choking on the bitter herbs they had cut—well, I wasn't feigning, I really was choking.

"We honor the values and traditions of our ancestors," I said, "and recognize that we are the product of their covenants. Because they believed in the future, because they were willing to bring forth children even in harsh times, and because they sacrificed their own comforts to afford their children better education and more opportunities than they had, we are who we are—indeed, we exist in the first place."

Dorothy nodded in agreement, and I continued: "In the course of maintaining these three covenants ourselves, we see changes that result from being in relationships over an extended period of time. We learn, for example, how to keep going even through hard times; we also learn to accept 'otherness,' whether the 'other' is a child or God; and we learn to trust—which means being vulnerable both to the people we love and the God we love. So keeping these covenants contributes directly to our relationship with eternity, that is, our covenant with God."

It was a late winter twilight many weeks later, with snow falling softly outside, when Dorothy neatly summarized this aspect of our talks:

Each covenant in time—future, present, and past—participates in the eternal covenant with God, so all of them mark our spiritual ways. We rarely focus on one covenant to the exclusion of the other two, but each one contains both expansive moments that transform the self and pain-filled moments that are inherent in love. (Is it an accident that one of the first words that babies learn is "bye-bye"?) We enter into deep commitments and then repeatedly suffer the pain of separation and loss. The older generation ages and dies, our children grow and leave us. Yet we know that our love can flourish only if we don't hold on but instead let go and allow love to prosper in freedom.

We couldn't possibly love and commit so deeply to any of our human covenants were it not for our covenant with God, which incorporates them all. It lifts them up and "holds" them even when we must release those we love. As a result, we face our vulnerability and our absurd tendency to fall completely and ever-hopefully in love, and in this absurdity lies the deepest wisdom. The Song of Songs really got it right: love is stronger than death—stronger than all our losses—and love is the way that most invitingly leads to God.

Dorothy ended the discussion:

> Love, as any parent can point out, is not a vague romantic word. Love means giving baths, folding diapers, playing catch, answering a million questions, driving, comforting, commiserating—all the actions entailed in parenting. Love demands work, daily expression, caring, nurturing, whether the relationship is parent to child, child to parent, or intragenerational. And while the love between peers differs from the love in an unequal relationship, all love is an education in covenant.

It was a clear, snappy December day when Dorothy announced to me that this would be her last visit. I was shocked. "No," she said, "it's not that I don't have anything more to learn from you—or" (chuckle) "that I have nothing else to teach you. It's that I'm moving to the

Boston area." I longed to protest, but let her continue. The tale that followed seemed like someone's nightmare, not at all like a story from the life of my feisty friend.

Dorothy had had a fall and had blacked out very briefly, although she didn't know which had come first. Her doctor, fearing she might have had a mild stroke, had her undergo a CT scan and an MRI. Both came out negative, but the incident upset her and greatly frightened Sammy and Joan. Suddenly she felt she had become an "unperson"— a problem to be solved. Sammy and Joan had long, private talks about her with her doctor and then told her that she'd be much better off living near them so they could look in on her regularly and be close by in case of emergency. Sammy told her quite forcefully—for him— that she had to move from her apartment in New York to one near them in Newton Centre, Massachusetts, a quiet suburb of Boston. There was a three-room apartment available two blocks from them, near shopping and near the trolley line that ran into town (by which they meant Boston).

> They were not going to take no for an answer, so after giving it plenty of thought over the next few days, I decided they were probably right. I will doubtless have more falls, and with my osteoporosis, it's only a matter of time before I break a hip. And that's without considering the macular degeneration and the other accumulated ills. I also figured that being eccentric as I am, I would be better off with people who knew and accepted my quirks than with hired home care. Then there's the chance to see my little ones much more often than now and forge a stronger relationship with them. I have to believe that Sammy, whom I've raised with such love and care, is really making the most thought-through and caring decision for my future.
>
> In a different culture, when people stayed in the same village for life, I might have been allowed to slip quietly and gently into plagues nine and ten. But now, I'm a city mouse forced to move to the country, and by gosh, I'm going to grow from the experience.

Not long after her move, Dorothy moved again, to a nearby assisted living facility. She has now been there for five years, with no further falls or blackouts, but her vision is almost gone. We speak on the phone about once a month, picking up each time where we had left off. She's been taking informal piano lessons from one of the other "inmates," as she calls them, and regularly leads group singing. The others are always amazed at how many songs she knows and, especially, how she knows all the lyrics by heart ("When I was performing, I certainly couldn't use sheet music"). She enjoys the grandchildren more and more as they grow older, and they think she's just grand. She remains cheerful and able to see the humor in her situation. For example, she mentioned that the food was all healthy but was cold by the time it reached her table—except the ice cream. There were advantages, she remarked, to having been a poor cook: "I never got used to gourmet meals."

I started to commiserate with her about her environment, but for the first time since I'd known her, she cut me off:

Was it Oscar Wilde (I love that man) who wrote—no, it was Richard Lovelace—never mind: "Stone walls do not a prison make, / nor iron bars a cage." I am not in Egypt, or, even if I am in Egypt, it's not in me.

As I listened to her familiar voice over the phone, I recognized school is not yet out: there are still lessons for me to learn from Dorothy, even in this supposedly unproductive time of her life.

3

DAVID
Mourning a Stillborn Daughter

David was referred to me for spiritual guidance by his rabbi because he had experienced a great loss and needed to discuss the process of mourning. We have all lost people close to us, but there is nothing generic about grief. Our individual reactions to loss develop out of the many choices and events that have shaped us over a lifetime. David's response, I would learn, combined a strong emotional sensitivity with a quirky intellectual curiosity.

A married, twenty-five-year-old supplier of plumbing goods, David was clearly upset when he came to see me one beautiful June day. His knock on my door was so faint that I was not sure I'd really heard it. And although outside the sky was bright, trees and flowers in Washington Square Park were in full bloom, toddlers were toddling, and birds were feasting on a scattering of crumbs left by a kindly park denizen, David's drawn face, his sad brown eyes, his sallow complexion, and his tall, slightly bent frame all combined to exude pure gloom. The reason quickly became clear: He had, several months earlier, buried Shoshana, a stillborn daughter that he referred to as his "first child." Moreover, his wife, Janice, was told that another pregnancy would put her own life at risk.

He went through the bare facts of his story in a monotone: how happy he and Janice were when she got pregnant; how thrilled they were to see the ultrasound pictures; and how Janice had had no sign of any problem. Everything changed in the ninth month, when the doctors said they had to induce labor immediately.

For more than a year, my task was simply to "hold" David. I made no attempt at explanations, sensing that I could help him most by just being present and listening to the anger, the sorrow, and the guilt that poured out of him. We live with our wounds, and David's injury would someday be less raw, although it would never disappear. But as the loss recedes in time, we gain strength and find that we can move beyond palliation to the difficult and painful work of mourning. And unbelievable as it may seem in the first pangs of grief, mourning our losses can be a creative process.

Because different family members mourn at different rates and in a variety of ways, grief often fails to bring a family together and can actually thrust them apart. Those left behind may appear to be squabbling over a memento, but the argument is merely a symptom of a deeper anger, perhaps of unresolved sibling rivalry or, more often, of individual differences in dealing with loss. David and Janice's misfortune was creating tensions between them at a time when they needed each other's support the most. I hoped that my working with David would not only help bring him to some healing but also help mend the relationship between the couple.

David and Janice had followed a book that their rabbi had given them on Jewish mourning rituals and practices that have developed over the centuries. It offered close guidance through the shivah—the week of deep mourning—and through the rest of the first month. It gave further information about the succeeding months of bereavement and ended with the *yahrzeit*, the anniversary commemorating the death. But it did not deal with the inner realities that David was confronting. Nor did it say anything about what would happen after the *yahrzeit*. Mourning is deemed to end after one year, and beyond that we are supposed to move on. But for many people it can take longer than that. Just as Dr. Benjamin Spock's *Baby and Child Care* offers advice up to a point and leaves us with no manual to navigate the adult years, so Jewish tradition stops at the anniversary. After that we are supposed to move on. Do we reread old letters? Dream of returning to earlier days? Or talk to the departed loved one and continue the conversation? What happens with the new space in our lives?

The books of the Hebrew Bible present moments of stark truth—such as King David's grieving the death of his son Absalom, who had even fomented a rebellion against his father. In describing the death of Sarah, Abraham's wife and Isaac's mother, only the immediate grief is mentioned. The text tells us that Isaac loved his wife Rebekah "and thus found comfort after his mother's death" (Genesis 24:67). But surely he also suffered some aftereffects: How did his mother's death affect Isaac's relationship with Rebekah? With his own children? Did Isaac never long for his mother's warmth and wisdom?

In another case, however, the text provides clues to the long-range effects of death. As described in Genesis, Judah was radically tempered by the consecutive losses of two sons. Judah, a son of the patriarch Jacob, joined with his brothers to sell Joseph, their youngest brother and Jacob's favorite, into slavery, allowing their father to believe that he had been killed by a wild animal. Judah subsequently married and had three sons. The first married Tamar but died because he displeased God. Judah then had his second son marry Tamar, but he, too, died. Judah then refused to allow a third son to marry Tamar, fearing that he would meet the same fate. So Tamar disguised herself, seduced Judah, and became pregnant with twin sons. At that point, Judah admitted that "she is more in the right than I, inasmuch as I did not give her to my son Shelah" (Genesis 38:26). (And as if to echo his judgment, one of the twins, Perez, becomes a forefather of King David.) Much later, Judah and his brothers traveled to Egypt seeking food during a famine. Joseph, who had risen to become vizier, disguised himself and took their youngest brother, Benjamin, as a hostage. Judah, having suffered the deaths of two sons himself, realized what a tremendous blow it would be for Jacob to lose his youngest son, so he offered himself up as a replacement for

Benjamin. (The story ends happily, as Joseph reveals himself and forgives his brothers with the words, "Although you intended me harm, God intended it for good" [Genesis 50:20].)

During our first session, I noticed David's eyes darting about, seeking (desperately?) something to focus on other than me. He settled on the abstract painting on the wall of my office. A year later, he was still speaking more to the painting than to me. I had not been surprised at David's numbness in reaction to the stillbirth. But the numbness persisted, even beyond the traditional Jewish year of mourning. The only sign he gave of trying to move beyond the tragedy and let God back into his life was that he kept showing up for spiritual guidance, never missing a session or even coming late. We looked at psalms of mourning and psalms of anger, but David never allowed his own feelings to emerge—he kept the conversation going only at a distance. I did not confront him directly about his lack of involvement with life and with the healing process, because doing so would have interfered with his need to discover his own path to reconciliation with God. Instead, I stayed out of the way, hoping that that would allow him to discern God's will, which seemed like a stationary cloud, hovering over David but just out of his reach. Nothing appeared to be happening, but later I could see that God's undemanding presence had held David far more securely than any person could have.

David continued to dream of Shoshana. He visualized her as she had looked when the nurse had washed her, dressed her, and allowed him to hold her. When I asked him if he felt he could love another child, he responded that he did love his niece and nephews. Yet he still had to grapple with why this happened and how he and his wife were to move forward. Together they had attended a support group for couples who had lost children, but the other couples had very different issues that didn't address David and Janice's needs. One man was blaming himself for his son's fatal bicycle accident, accusing himself of murdering his son; his wife protested, but not convincingly. A woman whose young daughter was run over by a speeding car couldn't get beyond her blind anger at the driver. After attending two sessions, David and Janice stopped going. It had now taken some sixteen months before the questions that were nagging David began to materialize:

> What did her life mean? Why was she born, only to not live? What did that mean? Years ago, in discussing my Mom's death, my Dad told me that no one ever died to teach someone else a lesson. So what value did her life have? Or maybe the whole thing was just an accident and there's no sense to it at all. But if that's so, why should I believe that my own life makes any sense? Either it all makes sense, or none of it does.

"What if it makes sense," I replied, "but we don't have the perspective or consciousness to take in the meaning? Sometimes we face events and must admit that we just don't know. I realize that this answer provides little satisfaction, but at least it's an honest one. I'm uncomfortable with religions that try to tidy up the messy edges. We don't know why some lives are long and others all too brief. We don't know why some people enter the world with birth defects that prevent them from living as fully as others."

David said, "I know. Someone even told me that I should be glad Shoshana died, because if she had lived she would have suffered greatly."

"Did that help?" I asked.

"Not at all. It didn't explain why she had any defect in the first place."

I told him I wanted to explain what I meant about not having perspective. There is a nineteenth-century novel by Henry Abbott called *Flatland*. It's a kind of geometrical romance that explains what reality would look like if we were all two-dimensional figures and a three-dimensional figure entered our world.

David furrowed his brow. "I don't get you," he said.

I clumsily drew some triangles, a square, and a pentagon on a sheet of paper and told him to imagine that they were people. "Look," I said, "you are like a super being—you can actually see their insides!"

I then made a fist, which David agreed was a solid object, in three dimensions. By lowering and raising my fist next to the table, that is, through the plane of the paper, I showed him that Mr. Fist could enter and leave Flatland at will. Flatlanders, for whom up and down do not exist, would perceive him only when he crossed their plane— materializing out of nowhere, starting as a point, growing larger, then smaller, and then disappearing, only to reappear somewhere else in their world if I performed the same motions next to a different side of the table. "Do you see that Flatlanders have a much more limited perspective than we have?" I asked.

"Yes," David said, understanding my point—in spite of himself, I thought—"but my question isn't about triangles and squares. It's not even intellectual." He turned away to avoid looking me in the eye. "I think it's emotional," he said with some embarrassment, staring determinedly at the painting on the wall.

A month went by before I saw David again. He had read *Flatland*, which he found in a library, and he had apparently gotten interested in another book he found there, a high school science textbook that discussed, among other topics, various theories about space. I was delighted that he was showing some signs of life and keenly sensed that some change or growth had taken place. For the first time since I'd met him, he was expressing curiosity about something other than death, or suffering, or justifying God's ways—or at least that is how it seemed to me at the time. He had read something about the universe constantly expanding and the curvature of space, which he didn't understand, but it got him thinking about space. If the universe is expanding, what is it expanding into, if not more space? Anyway, he reasoned, space must be infinite, because if it had an end or border, what would be beyond the border? Again, more space. He thought he was onto something. I listened closely while he invited me to enter his process of thinking about space.

I was reminded of an incident years ago, when an undergraduate student came to see me in a very agitated state. She said she had to talk to me at once to discuss the origin of the world. From experience I knew that every question of such magnitude is, ultimately, a personal one. She revealed that the evening before, she had learned that her parents were going to get divorced. She had spent the rest of the night on the ledge outside her dorm window, trying to decide whether or not to jump. We talked about her world, which was falling apart, and the larger world. Over the course of an hour, her parents' separation and impending divorce shrank from mythic, world-destroying proportions to a very sad event she could indeed mourn and still survive. (I then walked her to the counseling center.)

Whatever David's thinking about space had to do with his grieving process, my job was to be present and to help him become aware of God's presence as he moved forward in his life. David was a plumbing supplier, not a scientist or mathematician, so I knew that his interest in space did not derive from his work. Worlds are made up of space and time, so I guessed that he was rethinking and reconfiguring part of his world. David's central problem was how to shape a world that would be meaningful. As intrigued as I was, I kept reminding myself that the question he posed for himself was not primarily a cognitive concern. Somehow space would be his way of healing from his terrible loss. He continued:

> If space is infinite, then it must contain everything there is in the universe. Something can't fall out of the universe any more than we can fall off the edge of the earth. So since the universe is all there is, nothing can ever be lost. I guess it's a modern way of saying we're in God's hands. And if you add to that what I learned in high school, that matter and energy cannot be destroyed, only transformed one into the other, you get the physical equivalent of "nothing is ever really lost."

"So Shoshana isn't lost?" I asked.

> She may not be lost altogether, but she's still lost to me. Her matter may be taking on new forms, but she is not the baby who would have become a child, and then a teenager, and then an adult. Space won't do it.

"I don't know, though, if you should give up on space entirely," I said. "I believe you're thinking in the right direction. There are different types of space—emotional space, for example. Does Shoshana still occupy the same emotional space she did a year ago, last September?"

David looked to the painting, as if for help in answering my question. "No," he finally said, "not exactly."

I allowed that losing her and losing the chance to ever have a biological child had brought about a cataclysmic reshaping of his world. "You've spent more than a year choking on the debris of the catastrophe, but you now feel it would be useful to look around and sense what your new emotional landscape looks like."

David turned back to me. "But I haven't forgotten her," he said, quickly.

"And you shouldn't. Just as nothing can fall out of the universe, so, I would add, nothing that matters to someone is ever forgotten. We don't heal from grief by forgetting. We all walk through life with the many wounds we have suffered, but also with the new growth that emerges up around the site of the loss." He considered that for a while.

> So I'll never forget Shoshana, and if we were to adopt, another child wouldn't replace her. Actually, Janice and I have started to talk about adopting, and just the idea that we could have another child has cheered us both up. But it still doesn't explain . . .

His voice trailed off. After I saw that he was not going to finish the thought, I said, "I've told you from the start that I don't have answers. But I'm intrigued by your thoughts about space, especially the question of borders. But instead of asking what lies beyond space, what do you think is the border between life and death?"

David thought for a moment, his gaze now turning to the painting instinctively.

> I want to say that the dead we bury and the living we feed and take care of—but that's too simple. I guess what you're driving at is that death isn't some foreign country; that we've known it

all our lives; that it lives within us even as we imagine it to be outside of us trying to get in.

I told David that I thought that was a particularly useful insight on which to end the session. He got up to leave, and I noticed him taking one last, quick look at the painting.

Another month passed, and when David showed up in a winter coat, I wondered what had happened to fall. I was seeing ten seminary students that semester for spiritual guidance, each of them once a week, so I had had some forty sessions since I'd seen him last. I'd frankly forgotten where we had ended the previous time, but fortunately, he picked up right away where we'd left off. He looked very different from the way he looked when he had first come to see me. His eyes were lively, his walk brisk, and the stoop in his shoulders was gone. He launched right into his subject:

We were talking last time about the border between life and death. I always wondered why religious authorities debated when a fetus was viable. I thought it was a technical question—that when our premature intensive care improved, we'd push back the time of viability. But really the question is about this border between life and death, only now it's from the other end. When did Shoshana become alive and when did she die? Was she alive before Janice knew she was pregnant? Was she only potentially alive? And who died: Shoshana, or an *idea* of Shoshana, made up of all our hopes and dreams? From the state's point of view, she didn't die, because she never lived. From their perspective, I've spent a year and a half mourning a nonperson. And if she hadn't come to term, even Jewish law wouldn't have prescribed a funeral. But from the perspective of modern physics, I'm mourning someone who couldn't not be, because there is no "out of the universe." From the perspective of emotional space, as you call it, Shoshana, or our idea of Shoshana, created a space in our marriage and our lives in which to place a new life. That space is now empty.

"Do you think you might someday recognize the space created by Shoshana as an opportunity to serve others?" I asked.

"Maybe," he said, "but dammit, I still don't see the meaning of her life."

"I doubt that you'll ever see it," I replied. "All we can do is be creative, take risks, and trust that there is meaning beyond what we can know. If life weren't meaningful, why would you want to bring another life into the world?"

"So we're back to our 'easy' question: What is the meaning of life?"

"No," I said, "it's not easy, but it can be simple. The meaning of life is so simple that a child could know it—and so simple that a parent could overlook it completely. It hinges on the questions, Do you trust God or don't you trust God? Do you bet on life or don't you bet on life? And the Torah tells us, 'So therefore choose life.' It's all there— the blessings and the curses, and it's up to us to choose life."

I should have expected his response:

> And that's what we were doing in wanting to have a baby, but we were turned away. I'm hoping that we'll have the courage to do it again. Janice and I have become friendly with a couple who adopted a son. It took them many months and a lot of cash, but they couldn't be happier. We're trying to screw up our courage enough to talk to some adoption agencies. The process sounds a hundred times more difficult than getting pregnant—something can go wrong every step of the way, even after you already have the child.

David thanked me for what he described as listening to him for a year and a half. He thought he was reconciled to his loss now and wouldn't be coming back. I told him to please keep in touch and to feel free to see me any time he thought it would be useful. He took one last look at the painting on my wall and turned to leave. "Oh, and Janice says to please say thank you for her," he said.

The following winter, David phoned to tell me that they had adopted an infant girl, whom they had brought home two days ago, and asked if I would attend their baby-naming ceremony. I said I'd be thrilled.

At the end of the Book of Job, Job is given a new family twice as large as the old one, but perceptive readers of the text have long recognized that a new family cannot replace an earlier one. Job is not healed because he starts a new family; rather, he can start a new family because, to a sufficient degree, he has been healed.

4

STANLEY

A Psychologist Explores
Spiritual Guidance

A student I had seen for short-term spiritual guidance had a psychologist friend named Stanley who wanted to meet me to get a taste of the process. Stanley called me one day, and we arranged to meet over lunch. We got together in a quiet vegetarian restaurant in Greenwich Village, a few blocks from my school. He was not much taller than I—about five foot six, I'd guess—and looked to be in his early fifties, although he had maintained a certain boyish appearance and seemed to have the enthusiasm of a much younger man. He also projected an intensity that one often sees in people who are earnestly searching for answers to basic questions.

I was relieved that he never mentioned my student, because if he had, it would have led to some awkward sidestepping on my part. Stanley is in private practice and also teaches at a college. As we waited for the food to arrive, he asked me what exactly was involved in spiritual guidance. I assumed that he wanted to find out whether I was "practicing without a license." When I began to explain my background, he said, "Don't be defensive." (Ouch!) "I do know the difference between psychotherapy and spiritual guidance," he continued, "and that's why I'm coming to you." He told me that he was Jewish, that he had been a successful psychotherapist for twenty years and expected to continue in practice "till they drag me away." Some of the issues that had arisen in therapy sessions with his patients, though, and some of his own experiences ("I probably should have mentioned that first," he said, smiling) had raised spiritual questions for him. Not all psychotherapists are anti-religion, he told me. He, personally, believed that Sigmund Freud was profoundly religious—in the manner of the prophets—but had been misunderstood. He continued:

> Let me explain what I mean about spiritual questions. Many patients bring me their fears and insecurities, and their problems can be mitigated if I can help them understand the meanings that underlie the fears. But I've had a few patients who were looking for the meaning of all those meanings. These patients want to know what life is all about. "I've lived, and what does it all mean?"

Stanley said that he finds the religious vision in Freud's *Beyond the Pleasure Principle* to be in the direct line of Isaiah. I thought I knew what he meant but asked him to explain anyway, since he might have had something entirely different in mind. He said that he sees two sides to Freud. One is the physician, the familiar Freud whom psychotherapists study and who wanted to help people feel better. It is this Freud who, in his earlier years, wrote *The Future of an Illusion*, in which he calls religion a wish, or an illusion. Ever since, mainstream psychology has thought of religion as a crutch that people use until they become healthy.

But the second side, Stanley believed, was Freud the *metaphysician*, who struggled with trying to determine what reality must be like if talking to him could cure people of their neuroses. In *Beyond the Pleasure Principle*, which he wrote late in life, Freud divides reality into two forces, Eros (love) and Thanatos (death). Warming to his subject, Stanley continued:

> He actually quotes a passage from the Book of Isaiah in which God says, "I form the light and create darkness; I make peace,

and create evil." Freud knew what Isaiah already knew two thousand years ago, that we must accept and integrate the whole shebang—the bad with the good, the misery with the pleasurable, the darkness with the light.

Stanley explained that it has long been fashionable to debunk Freud, even before his blatantly sexist views were recognized, because he used a very specialized group of cases—he dealt with upper-middle-class Viennese, especially Jews, in the early twentieth century—from which he generalized about everyone everywhere. What these critics don't realize is that they are rejecting only the first Freud while tacitly and wholly accepting the much more important second side, the worldview on which all talking therapy is based.

But I'm not troubled by psychotherapists' widespread hostility to religion because they're not attacking the god I believe in. My God respects me, my individuality, and my attempts to grow. Ironically, it was a Greek Orthodox writer, Nikos Kazantzakis, who best expressed what I believe is a very Jewish point of view: that religion isn't the harbor where we put down anchor, but the harbor from which we set sail.

As the waiter approached with our food, Stanley suddenly stopped himself, aware that he had been passionately lecturing. He dropped his voice down and asked, "Will you see me?" Of course I would, grateful for the chance to talk about Freud and all the other magnificent doctors of the mind. I promised myself to remember that the purpose of spiritual guidance is to foster the guidee's relationship with God and vowed not to focus my burning curiosity onto Stanley's views on—the list danced in my mind: Freud, Erich Fromm, Viktor Frankl, Abraham Maslow, Oliver Sacks—all those Jewish doctors searching for a new language to talk about meaning and the long process of becoming fully human. I did put one question to him, though:

"Psychotherapists are also human. Can you ask for help?"

"Right," he said. "Well, I *am* asking; the question really is whether I can come to you with the openness that I want to see in my patients."

We agreed to meet again, the following week in my office at the college. I suddenly wondered what my makeshift, windowless office would look like to a therapist. The only daylight it receives, when I prop open the door between seeing students, comes through the glass of an emergency exit down the hall labeled "This door is alarmed," to which someone had added, "Please don't upset it further." Above my desk hangs a poster commemorating the tercentennial of Spinoza's birth. On the desk itself are the computer and the telephone. Next to the desk, on my left, is an overflowing three-shelf bookcase. Above the chair that he would occupy hangs an abstract painting of a man's head, and on the wall next to that an abstract representation of the desert.

I had scheduled Stanley for the first hour of my day, at 9 A.M., and was surprised to find him waiting at my door when I arrived at about 8:40. Rush-hour traffic was stalled outside as usual, and the blare of a thousand taxi horns penetrated the emergency door. I couldn't leave him standing in the hall, so I had to ask him to step into my office, resenting that I couldn't have a few minutes to collect myself, look through my e-mail, and mentally prepare myself for speaking with him. So our first formal meeting began awkwardly. Also, I was aware that he had certain therapeutic expectations and had his own accustomed way of structuring a session. I was determined to keep myself out of the discussion—this was not about my being impressed or inhibited by his psychological expertise. I began as I always do, with my two ground rules: (1) anything said here between us stays in this room, and (2) the guidee sets the agenda.

Stanley agreed, and we sat in silence for a few moments as I waited for him to begin. I was staring demurely, I thought, at the floor when I noticed that he was nervously flexing and unflexing his toes inside his shoes. He had taught himself not to display his emotions while he was with patients, and here he was, displaying the same kind of signal he himself would have noticed in an instant.

We both felt the quietness in the room. Stanley remarked on it, then said he wasn't sure whether to start by describing his family of origin, his present sense of unease, or his intellectual curiosity. Then he simply started talking. Almost immediately, Stanley the psychotherapist disappeared, and Stanley the man, loving and being loved, came to the fore. His initial psychological training had disparaged religion because his teachers subscribed to the "crutch" theory. Psychoanalysts, he was taught, should be able to see through the security blanket of religion to the illusion it "really" is and to carry on without the comfort of religious doctrine. Within that context, he felt no inclination to defend religious practices and beliefs. He had, he said, treated many patients who were badly wounded by the teachings, rules, and judgments of one denomination or another.

> I had one patient, a lovely, gentle young man, who was convinced he was guilty of murder. It seems that he masturbated regularly, and since the rules of his religion did not distinguish potential life from actual life, he felt guilty for all the "spilt blood" that resulted from his habit. He would wash his hands with the hottest water he could but believed, like Lady Macbeth, that he could never remove the bloodstains. The pain caused by the hot water was justified retribution for his sin, he said, even if it could not expiate it or even stop him from committing the same sin again the next day.

For many years, Stanley was ready to write off religion as more pernicious than good.

> Oh, I know all the great altruists and saints who overcame inhuman odds through faith, but I could counter them with endless lists of holy wars, pogroms, homophobia, racism, sexism, and all sorts of belittling and demeaning behavior in the name of religion.

"They've taken what you love and distorted it," I ventured. He paused, considered, and responded:

Yes, that's right. In part I'm angry because I know that's not what religion is or should be about. When I'm working with some patients, I really feel that I'm on holy ground. They may come in hurt by the strictures of religion, and yet religion, at its best, has opened me to perceive the holiness in and through them. I am called to work with them, to take urgent calls at night, to walk with them through some of the most difficult times of their lives, because each life has such essential dignity and value. In some cases when I'm with a patient I sense a Presence—I even feel guided. For example, last month I was talking with a patient who has metastasized cancer. She had had two previous bouts with cancer and seemed to be making a good recovery each time, but this time it is inoperable. Her dignity and strength in the face of this diagnosis are really awesome. She is determined to use the time that remains to make sense of her life. She isn't working with me to overcome depression or a sense of victimization. She is hoping I can help her in the task of making some meaning out of her life.

I nodded, noting that we had obviously experienced similar feelings in our work.

It's clear I'm doing what I should be doing, but it's also clear that I want to do more. After my patients are healed, mobile, moving further out in their lives, they are still a locus for God's actions—

He stopped suddenly, embarrassed at having invoked God, flexed and unflexed his toes furiously, and looked to me for a reaction. I said that "God" was not an uncomfortable word in our context. "Spiritual guidance is supposed to help us gain a deepening intimacy with God."

Spiritual guidance remains a process I don't fully understand and don't really control. It describes a way of both being with the guidee and, at the same time, becoming invisible so that the person can experience God's presence. The focus must always be on God, not on some remark I make. He repeated, almost to himself, "Deepening intimacy with God. That's scary." All intimacy is initially scary, but it is also life's greatest value. Even more than wanting to know, we want to be known. As our session was drawing to a close, he said, "OK, what should I read? think about? Do you examine dreams?" I reminded him of our second rule: This is your time to use as you wish.

On his next visit, Stanley had hardly settled into his chair when he asked, "Can I talk about what happened with me with one of my patients?" I told him that this wasn't supervision but his time to use as he pleases. He considered what I said and then continued:

> I know it isn't supervision—and it's because of experiences like those I've had with this woman that I came to see you. I've been seeing Sarah for four months. Leaving aside my diagnosis, I found her unappealing. She's overweight, her face is broken out, her hair sort of hangs there, and the physical reality expresses her whole affect as well. She seems to sit there saying, "Take advantage of me." I was angry with myself for not liking her more—not really connecting. I soon found myself praying to love her, to see God in her. Now, you may do that all the time, but that was a first for me. I didn't even know I'd remembered how to pray. I prayed while she sat across from me—I simply looked down at my desk and let the words form in my head. Then, as I slowly lifted my head and turned to her, she looked different! It was that sudden, that startling. I cared. Deeply. I think she felt it too.

"The way you felt the sudden quietness in the room last time you were here?" I asked.

He looked surprised but then said simply, "Yes. You probably get this all the time—people telling you that praying made a difference."

"No—not all the time, and there's nothing magical or controllable about it. But I can't do it alone, without calling on God. I also know that what happens here emerges from the guidee's relationship to God."

> I was going to ask you whether I'd still be interested in Sarah
> when I next see her, but I know that's not my question. What I
> really want to know is how to enter fully into this deep part-
> nership—relationship—to Sarah that's necessary for me to help
> her. I want to help, I want to heal. I spent a few months telling
> myself all the reasons I should sympathize with her: her domi-
> neering father, her neglectful mother, her several failed relation-
> ships. But I couldn't get beyond my visceral aversion to her, even
> though I explored what she triggered in me—whom she might
> be reminding me of. After just a few seconds of prayer, though,
> the whole relationship changed.

I let silence fill the room for a full half minute, until the blaring air
horn of a truck penetrated both the "alarmed" door and the heavy
metal door to my office. The spell broken, I asked him, "Do you want
to learn how to be a better healer, or do you want to be open to the
presence of God?"

Stanley rolled his eyes.

> I should know by now that my techniques of healing don't
> always work. I guess in this case I need to—how did you put it
> last time?—help her gain a deepening intimacy with God. OK,
> I'm in for the long haul.

He continued talking about Sarah, assuring me that that wasn't
her real name. She had told him she came to him because she was
depressed, life was passing her by, and nothing seemed to matter to
her. He was still trying to get her to identify her feelings more specifically and begin relating them to feelings she had had earlier in her
life. It was going more slowly than he was comfortable with, and he
was sure that his negative feelings about her were hindering her
progress, however hard he tried to hide them.

We agreed to meet monthly until further notice. When I saw him
next, his clothes were more casual than before. A good sign, I
thought. He's getting more comfortable with me. He began, "Do peo-

ple ever use this like a confessional?" I explained that there weren't
"people," there was only him, and this was his time to use as he chose.
"Well, OK then, I have a problem with a boundary issue."

Uh, oh!—I liked Stanley and looked forward to seeing him, but
that phrase "boundary issue" set off all my alarms. "Boundary issue"
has become the bland way professionals describe overstepping the
privilege of working with vulnerable people. It almost always signals
an exploitative sexual relationship, and I knew from past experience
that my sympathy for the victim always trumps my relationship with
a guidee. Where was his "holy ground" now? I kept staring at my desk
and said to myself, "God, help me to help him. I like him, I liked him,
but I won't be able to work with him if the problem is a boundary
issue."

It's possible that Stanley didn't notice my turmoil, because he
continued in the same measured tone.

My brother and his family live in Colorado. We get together
maybe twice a year, either there or here in New York. But his
daughter, Janice, just started college in the city. She came to see
me last month. She's a very likable kid, but the move to New
York has been hard for her. I took her to dinner, and she immediately began pouring out her problems. My brother wanted her
to major in something practical: business, economics, interna-
tional relations—anything that would help her get a job and
career going when she graduated. She, however, was attracted by
theater, music, fine arts—all disciplines that would draw on her
creativity. I enjoyed playing the role of caring uncle, but she
wanted more. I know I shouldn't have, but I agreed to see her,
and before I knew it, I was seeing her twice a week, and she was
telling me things about my brother and sister-in-law. Now I'm
not sure how to get out of it. I hate the role I've gotten into, but
she's progressing so well and—

Thank you, God, the boundary issue is one of treating a member
of the family. I can still care for him and help him. If she was, in fact,

doing well, she could be referred. He had been in the psychological community for twenty years, so surely he knew some people who could treat her. And if money was an issue, he could still be the caring uncle and help pay her bills. We talked a little about this. I expressed my surprise that he hadn't referred her to someone else sooner, but then I sensed this was all a smoke screen before we got to his larger question.

As he was talking about his niece and her artistic fervor, it became clear to me that he was really talking about himself. So I asked him how he happened to get into psychology and what was going on now in terms of his self-understanding.

Stanley was embarrassed to see how transparently his own career journey had mirrored his niece's. His father, too, had wanted him to study something practical in college, though in his day, practical meant history, or government, or something he could teach on the high school level.

In my freshman year, I took an introductory psych course. I was fascinated by the thought of hearing people's stories and helping them find their way. When I announced to my parents that I was going to major in psychology, all my father said was, "They don't teach that in high school." I took the GREs, and to my great surprise, I not only got into my first-choice school, but they gave me a fellowship that covered tuition and basic expenses. That was great, because my parents were against my going to grad school and it would have been hard to ask them for financial support. I know I made the right choice going into psychology. I didn't agree with all my professors, but working under their supervision was really valuable.

As a future clinician, I had to undergo therapy myself, and the school had a special grant that covered the expense. It wasn't fun, but it was probably the single most important experience of my graduate training. After I got my degree, I worked for a while in a city agency and slowly began to build up a private practice. I've been in practice now for twenty years. I like what I'm doing, but I don't think it's all I'm called to do. I guess "called to" is a funny expression, but I have the clearest sense that I'm a little too settled, too comfortable. My initial feeling back in freshman year, that I wanted to help people find their way, is still true, but I sense that I'm being asked to do it in a deeper way.

It was clear that Stanley was called, but to what? I sensed that he was called to explore a painful distinction he faced: between religion as an illusion, as he had been taught, and religion as a profound insight. He thought he drew the distinction because his own experiences were moving him beyond complacency. At a time when he enjoyed success, stability, financial reward, and respect in his field, he was not looking for change, but he felt he was being called. Calls can come at times of pain (pain can be a trumpet), but his was coming at a time of satisfaction.

"And don't bother looking for earthquakes in my life," he said. "My wife agrees that there have been no major changes in the last few years that could account for this circumstance." Nor, he said, were these feelings the first warning tremors of aging and questions of mortality. They had come in a time of fullness, not need; satisfaction, not incompleteness; personal joy, not fear or sorrow.

I replied that the call is ongoing—most people attend to it only out of desperation. "But you are able to hear and pay attention to the call even on a sunny day, when all that surrounds you could lull you into sleep or complacency."

"How should I respond to the call?" he asked.

"As you are already doing: learning how to attend, that is, being open and aware with no preconceived idea of what might emerge without your actively seeking it. Also, testing out your sense of direction by discussing it with someone and maintaining your regular practice, which has brought you this far. Do you follow any regular spiritual practice?" I asked.

Well, actually, since that moment when I found myself praying for Sarah, I began praying in a few regular ways: I say a prayer on awakening each morning; I pray for clarity and that I do no harm to each of my patients; then I say another prayer just before going to sleep—using that as an opportunity to review the day. I began by using the Jewish prayer book but soon found my mind drifting, so now I use it only when I can't get my own prayer thoughts going.

Stanley wondered whether other psychotherapists have touched the holy in and through their work. He toyed with the idea of running a session at a local professional meeting, but he wasn't quite ready for that. Instead, he decided to talk one-on-one with a colleague with whom he felt he could broach the subject. He then went into a tirade against God-language:

The name with the greatest emotional horsepower has been co-opted by people whose goals are antithetical to God's. We see the God of liberation, of growth, of authenticity—and they give us God the policeman, the dictator, the narrow-minded, judgmental—

Again he stopped himself, and we were both smiling once more as his love of God took the form of fury against those who had perverted the use of that sacred name for their own political ends. We talked about how his own God-image had been formed. He had grown up with the typical childhood image of God as a combination of parent, policeman, rabbi, teacher, Superman, and grandfather, but he had stayed in Hebrew school long enough to be exposed to the God of the prophets. In college he had learned about Eastern religions, and although Buddhism held some initial attraction for him, he was far enough in his psychological studies to be uncomfortable with the idea of the no-self. The no-self, he said, relieves you of responsibility, because responsibility depends on there being a consistent self that learns from its previous actions and sees their effects in this world. Essentially, he had "bracketed" the God question until the day he caught himself praying.

"It is quite possible," he said, "to be involved in Jewish life, to keep the holidays, to sing the songs and support the community without ever thinking about God."

"But," I allowed, "you've left room for a relationship with God to grow within you—"

He nodded. "—and it looks as though God has taken up the invitation." He suddenly turned red.

> It sounds so *chutzpahdik*—nervy—but that's how I see it, too. It's as if God said, "You haven't been satisfied with any of the false gods, so I think you're ready for me to introduce myself." I feel a little the way I felt when I first met my wife. I'm excited and scared, and I know this is absolutely important and I want to say, "Yes, yes, yes!" but I know I'm not worthy. It's so big.

"It *is* big," I said, "and it's also everyday and ordinary. Discovering your wife and making the commitment was momentous, but over time, your relationship with her has helped structure your life, and it supports and anchors you. It no longer distracts you from your other work." I told him how, when I was teaching undergraduate students, I could always tell who was really in love and who was merely obsessed: those in love improved their grades and the others fell behind. He chuckled. I went on to say that the effect was even more true with the love of God: "Then shall your light burst through like the dawn . . ." (Isaiah 45:7).

"You love Isaiah too," he remarked. "I really do want everyone to see how Freud's *Beyond the Pleasure Principle* is like Isaiah's vision. I suppose I could lead a session at the psychological association."

I asked him if that was willingness or willfulness, that is, would he be responding to a call or shaping the situation to his needs? I could almost read his thoughts as I watched his face relax from a questioning frown into a half-smile of recognition.

> Good question. I suppose I'm trying to guess what I'm called to—and all I need to do is wait, be open, and, with your help,

discern what in fact I'm called to. It might turn out to be easier than I thought. I don't have to imagine; I just have to wait.

We compared notes on waiting: he with the intense waiting that grew up between him and a patient after a powerful insight, I with the milder but also important waiting when I asked a question in class. In my first year of college teaching, the pause between a question posed and an answer offered seemed interminable. I wanted to fill the silence with answers. I told him that I learned, instead, to count to myself, and never in thirty years of teaching had I ever counted higher than fifteen. I learned to yield control, to trust, and—to use a difficult term—"surrender." That seemed like a good word on which to end the session, so I stood up. He said, "Thank you," and made for the door awkwardly, trying not to turn his back on me. He bumped into the door, looked to see if I'd noticed, said "oops" pointedly, recovered his poise, and then left.

A month later, Stanley once again brought up *Beyond the Pleasure Principle*, specifically an experiment described in the book. Freud writes that he placed a single cell in a petri dish and noted that it died after a period of time. But when he put two cells into the petri dish, both lived much longer than the first had. Stanley mused on how, like the first cell, we can drown in our own juices. I asked him what this had to do with Isaiah, and he responded, "There are only two religions: the religion of openness and welcome, comfort and healing, and the religion of boundaries and condemnation, curses and war."

"You sound like a prophet."

He replied:

What would a modern-day prophet sound like? I've often thought that Freud was a true prophet—really. It's not that he wasn't ever mistaken, or even dogmatic, it's that he saw what others couldn't see. Prophets don't see into the future; they see the deepest meaning of the present.

I told Stanley that I also appreciated Freud's genius, but we weren't talking about Freud, we were talking about him. I noticed his toes flexing again.

> OK, I know, I heard you and I chose not to respond. Do you know how scary it is to be called a prophet, even in jest? Prophets don't die of old age. They don't develop hobbies or plant a garden in the suburbs.

"I didn't realize you lived in the suburbs and were an avid gardener," I said.

"I don't, and I'm not, but I could," he said.

"Who are some of the nonbiblical people you think of as prophetic?"

"My personal pantheon?"

"Well, pantheon is hardly the right term, but your top forty." He answered:

> It's funny, but the first one I think of is Mozart. I know he didn't write his own librettos, and we usually associate prophecy with words, but the deeper association is with truth, and Mozart's music is true—inevitable—it reminds us of values and goodness we once knew.

"Freud and Mozart. Any others?"

"Some of our poets—Chaim Nachman Bialik really speaks to me. I guess that's why people call them inspired. They see what we see, only deeper."

"Are you going to list artists?"

"Certainly Chagall."

"Do you see what you've done with prophecy? It's true that Mozart died young, but the poet you mentioned didn't, nor the artist. If you could be Mozart, or Bialik, or Chagall, would you find it so frightening to be a prophet?" I sensed a little light turning on inside him.

You know, we are all called, but some of us aren't listening. I certainly didn't listen for most of my life—up till now. To be a prophet is to be true—authentic—and to bring forth that truth. It's not necessarily about denouncing some particular government or crying doom, although that's the popular depiction. It's to see the depth dimension of things and to find a way to express it. Sometimes prophets are giants, like Isaiah, and Jeremiah, or, on my list, Mozart, Chardin—

How, I asked him, did the painter Jean Chardin get in there?

Chardin can paint a single onion, a scallion, or an empty glass, and somehow you never see these objects the same way again. I believe that prophecy didn't end with the biblical prophets. For some we may identify just one or two inspired moments, but the quest for truth is fresh and ongoing.

He paused, a bit shaken by his own fervor. We sat in silence for a while. Then he said:

Intensity is my middle name. I don't do things by half-measure. I guess a number of things scare and confuse me. I know I have passion, maybe even some truths, but I'm not an artist or a musician or a poet, and I certainly don't want to come across like one of those religious nuts on TV.

I reminded him that Mozart did not preach, nor Bialik, nor Chagall. They were true to their inspiration, and that was all they had to be. Another silence. Then:

I thought of another: van Gogh. I always loved his paintings, but then I read his letters to his brother. Van Gogh started out as a minister. He actually wrote in a letter that he wanted to paint people so that you could see the halos around them. He didn't literally want to paint a halo; he wanted to help us to see the inherent divinity of his subjects. He put into words a lot of what I'm feeling.

Do prophets ever give their insights one-on-one, as I do occasionally in therapy, or do they have to proclaim it to a whole city? In other words, does prophecy require a public, or is the truth of the vision enough?

"What do you do with Emily Dickinson," I asked, "who wrote and wrote but never published anything, didn't even leave her house for fifty years?"

"Wonderful!" he said. "She produced the poems—the prophecy, really—but left it to God to see that her messages eventually got out into the world. Oh, I like that."

"If you have no intention of deliberately going public but just want to write up your cases as you've always done, what difference does the title 'prophet' make?"

Look, all ground is holy, and when you know that, you walk with greater care. Even so, most of the time I'm not conscious of the holiness. It's the same with knowing that every person is in the image of God. I think if I were fully conscious of that, I couldn't ride up an elevator with a crowd of people. In quieter moments, certainly when I'm doing therapy, I let the awareness filter through. Then my eyes are wide open, and every move I make and everything I say, I do with the greatest awe and respect. If I add to that the sense that in some way I'm a prophet, well, it means as I write up my notes I recognize that I am writing a piece of sacred scripture.

He gave a nervous laugh. I raised an eyebrow, and he said:

OK. Back in the sixties, I read a great book, *A Canticle for Leibowitz*, by Walter Miller—do you know it? It's one of those post-nuclear books. A society has decided that some man named Leibowitz, whose corpse is one of the few remnants of the previous society, must have been a holy figure. They find a text in his pocket and believe it must be holy scripture—it's actually his shopping list.

"Can a shopping list really be sacred scripture?" I asked.

He thought for a while and then said, "The little notes we write ourselves can tell us what we value." He reached into his pocket and pulled out a handful of Post-its and other scraps of paper.

"Call about Mildred's medicine," he read out. "Get McDougall book." "Jack's phone number, but who's Jack?" "Update computer antivirus." "IRS." "Fat-free yogurt!" He read the last with great emphasis, to highlight how silly he thought it was. Then he continued:

When I reread the book recently, I realized that *Leibowitz* is not a post-nuclear book at all. Miller presents a situation in which some shred of the past has been taken as holy writ. But if it can be taken that way in the future, why not take it that way now? We could consider every piece of writing as holy writ; even more, we could regard every person and every utterance and every plant and animal as holy. The book simply uses its setting to help us recognize the wonder of what we have here and now—everything we have here and now. All my prophets are really saying the same thing: "It is good, it is very good."

Freud and Miller both want to show that we find holiness in the mundane details, the slips of the tongue, and the Post-its. God is in the details. We don't have the vision to take in vast designs, so we have to learn to notice the everyday world. I guess that's why I had Chardin on my list.

What I see in Freud and in most of his followers is a quest for wholeness, for healing, for a return to our essential status. Many of the important writers on psychotherapy use explicitly religious language. Abraham Maslow does, and Viktor Frankl talks about meaning. I guess since Freud we've all gotten uncomfortable with God-talk, and we'd never use the word "soul," but when we therapists are sitting focused on that empty space between the patient and ourselves, we know that it's not empty. And our awareness of that may be awareness of God.

We finished up the hour on more neutral ground, but I was concerned about our next meeting. Was Stanley's vision sustainable? After his patient load and simple human obligations, where would his thoughts be the next time I saw him? But when he walked through the door a month later, it was as if the conversation had never ended. He started right in:

OK, let me get down to the details. Since I last saw you, I've been doing everything I usually do, but it feels different—it feels less hurried (although fifty minutes are still fifty minutes) and it feels easier. I don't feel stressed. At the end of the day I'm tired—exhausted, actually. But during the day I feel alert and totally present. And the tiredness I feel, the exhaustion, is the same as what you feel after you've gone on a long hike, or totally cleaned up the garden. It is exhaustion that comes from using all of yourself, and you know sleep will be refreshing and easy. It's funny, after all this—it's all so simple.

We are called in different ways. Stanley was called through success, not loss, the more usual way. His call was to become a psychotherapist. But all calls have one thing in common: we are asked to be most fully who we are in our relationship with God.

5

ELI

The Meaning of Loneliness Within the Family

Eli was a successful banker, married more than twenty years, with three children: a daughter and a son, both away at college, and a younger son who was a senior in high school. He spoke warmly about his family, seemed to enjoy his work, and yet indicated that he felt lonely all the time. Like some of my other guidees, Eli had a rabbi who suggested that spiritual guidance might be just what the doctor ordered. I told him that I was neither a doctor of medicine nor a doctor of psychology, but a doctor of philosophy. I tried to reach out to him by making a lame joke: "People are always asking me, 'What kind of a sickness is philosophy?'" I immediately realized I'd taken the wrong tack when he reacted just enough to show me he understood the joke but it would be beneath him to acknowledge it by laughing. I soon realized that small talk of any sort was anathema to him.

Eli had a somewhat abstracted air about him, as though he were not totally present. His dark hair was tousled, not in the stylish way of the young, but like someone who neglects to keep his barbershop appointments. He had a furrowed brow that put his face into a perpetual frown. His clothes tended toward the somber and the formal: I never saw him without a jacket and tie. Altogether, he exuded nonstop tension, and I felt my own tension rising to meet his uneasiness. I asked him what brought him to see me.

> I feel lonely, very lonely—all the time. I like my work, I love my family, but I can't seem to get over this feeling of being alone, even when I'm with other people—well, especially when I'm with other people. I'm constantly at war with myself about this loneliness. On the one hand, I want to believe that it's something I inherited: my father's life was successful and rewarding, and yet he always complained of feeling lonely. On the other hand, I keep telling myself that if I'm lonely, I'm the only one who can do something about it.

Eli paused and looked around the room as if to see whether he'd said too much. Whatever he saw, or didn't see, seemed to satisfy him because he continued:

> My dad was a teacher, and whatever companionship he didn't get from his teaching colleagues he got from his students. I, on the other hand, work behind the scenes at a bank, and while I get along reasonably well with my coworkers, I'm not close with any of them. They often go out together for a drink after work, and I would feel like an outsider if I joined them. Besides, I'm really not like them. They're all "hail fellow, well met" types—and if they didn't work in the same office, I'd never be friends with any of them. And actually, I'm not. In fact, I have very few friends, and maybe that's why I'm lonely. On the other hand, I've been told I push people away and that I take everything too seriously. Well, I do—life is a serious business.

It was clear that he was conflicted: every thought he had seemed to have an "other hand." I remarked that there was nothing wrong with taking life seriously, that I surely did—that if I didn't, I wouldn't be doing spiritual guidance. I'm not the cheerleader type, I said; rather, I was committed to helping people find their own spiritual paths—ones that grow out of their own identities. I added, as I do with all my guidees, that the spiritual way is not an easy road to take, that he should be prepared to work hard in and out of his sessions with me. I then asked him, "Since when have you felt lonely?"

"Since when?" he repeated. "Good question, since when?" He shifted in his chair and fiddled with his tie. "Since when?" he said once more, to win a bit more time for searching his memory.

> I think it began in earnest when I was in junior high school. I was picked on for not joining in the other kids' horseplay and for wanting to do well in my classes. Somebody called me "Beanstudy," because I was skinny and preferred doing home-work to teasing girls. The epithet was soon shortened to "Beanstud," and it stuck. All through junior high, that's what the other kids called me, as though it was my name. I even learned to answer to it. High school wasn't much better. I was never really *in*—not that I wanted to be, with those kids. For most of them, studying and getting good grades were for nerds. Being serious was even worse, punishable by getting laughed at. I never stopped being serious, though, and I never learned how to make small talk, which is all everybody else wants to do. Actually, some of my classmates were really OK. They didn't tease me, but even they couldn't get interested in the questions I thought were important.
>
> The usual definitions of loneliness don't seem to apply to me—at least I can't quite explain it. I'm usually even more lonely when I'm with people than when I'm alone. I don't feel depressed, really, but this loneliness has lately gotten to be much more of a problem, and I'm hoping that you can help me.

Eli's wife thought he was coming to see me because of their impending "empty nest," something he said she was dealing with quite well. Sheila had gone back to work three years ago, he said, with a gardening firm. She loved plants and got up every morning looking forward to a pleasant day spent in doing what she loved to do. But he rejected the empty-nest idea vigorously. He described it as "too sim-plistic" to explain what he was suffering from, and indeed, I believed it was actually irrelevant to what he was trying to address, given that he had already felt lonely in his early teens. I reasoned that because he had first related his problem to his rabbi and then followed the rabbi's advice to see me, he sensed it was a religious issue at work. I told him that while his loneliness was uncomfortable, his present awareness of it indicated some genuine spiritual growth.

Over the course of the next few months, he continued to speak about loneliness, but some other ideas were creeping in. One especially frustrating day, after he'd gotten into what he admitted was a stupid argument with one of his coworkers at the bank about the cor-rect way to fill out a certain form, he began by essentially venting his disappointment:

> Expecting anything from other people takes from your inde-pendence and leaves you lonely when they disappoint you. Other people are hell. My boss takes me completely for granted—the only times I ever hear from him are when I've done something wrong, meaning something he doesn't like. My sister promised to pick up a *Time* magazine for me and then completely forgot about it. My next-door neighbor leaves his car parked in our joint driveway "only for a second," which turns into an hour.

I told him that his view of other people was shared by no less a personage than the French intellectual Jean-Paul Sartre, who had expressed the same idea in his play *No Exit*. I challenged him to decide whether he agreed with Sartre's worldview. He hadn't expected to be challenged and said, "I was just expressing my feelings," but I pressed the point. How, exactly, did he view other people?

After telling me that he'd read both Sartre and Marcel Proust, he repeated, "How do I view other people?" After a pause, he said, "I'll have to think about that." Again he was stalling for time: "You mean intellectually, not emotionally? How do I view other people?"

"Do you think you have one view intellectually and another emotionally?" I asked.

"Well, yes," he said, moving away from the original question.

> When I say intellectual, I mean rational, that is, carefully worked out, using our God-given reason. On the other hand, when I say emotional, it's what I believe when I'm not thinking. Isn't that what you mean?

The separation he described between reason and emotion and his earlier statement that he was saying not what he thought but how he felt, called forth another challenge. When, I asked, was he going to unify his mind and his heart?

He sidestepped that question, too, by saying that he'd really have to think about what he'd said to me about other people, but I suggested that it wasn't so much a question of what he said to me as what he said to himself. How was he *naming* his own experiences? Once again, he avoided my question, this time returning to the theme of "other people are hell" but relating an incident that gave him some hope:

> I have to say that there was one person I truly admired, though I barely knew him. He worked in our office a few months ago, basically came and went in about two weeks. I don't know if he was transferred or fired, or maybe he just quit. Anyway, the first time he came into the staff room at the bank for lunch, he sat down at the large table, waited for a lull in the conversation about last night's Yankee–Red Sox game, and then asked, addressing no one in particular, "So what do you think about death?" Now *there* was a conversation stopper, if I ever heard one. Like everyone else in the room, I first thought he was kidding around but then realized he was serious. And like my coworkers, I was dumbstruck. If no one else had been around, I would have gladly discussed death with him, but as it was, I felt embarrassed, conditioned by years of being told myself that I

was "too serious." His question was left hanging in the room, like a body swinging from a noose. It was incontrovertibly there, but nobody talked about it. Gradually the banal conversation reemerged, and soon the questioner was gone from the staff room, never to return. But there, I felt, went a kindred spirit.

I said we'd have to leave it there, but I'd see him again in a month. When I next saw Eli, he looked even more uncomfortable than I'd remembered. He went back to talking about his loneliness, but this time took the subject further, relating it to his spiritual search:

> Yes, the spiritual way is lonely, and I often feel I'm thinking in a vacuum about all the things I most care about. No one really understands what I'm going through: my coworkers think I'm unfriendly, my kids think I'm just the quiet type, and Sheila has pegged me as moody and worrying in advance about empty-nest syndrome. The prayer book and the psalms always talk about finding solace in God. I say the words, and I'm sure some people do find comfort in God, but I can't seem to do it. I should add that I do believe in God; on the other hand, I can't get myself to believe that God is worried about *me*.

Eli had, by this time, worked himself into a state. His voice was well above the decibel level needed to carry across the five feet that separated us. The fervor of his outburst suggested that he was homing in on what his loneliness embodied. I pointed out that the vehemence of his remarks was important because it showed how passionately he felt about his relationship with God and that his discontent gave us something to work with. He was surprised to hear that I was actually pleased he had "lost control," as he put it. I explained that it was real progress to move from blaming others to accepting his own self-dissatisfaction.

He felt the loneliness most keenly when he addressed the questions that interested him: "Does life have any meaning?" "If so, how should I be living?" "Is there a God who cares about me?" and "Am I really free, or am I simply living out God's plan?" I told him that philosophers beginning with Socrates had grappled with pretty much the same questions. Yes, he said, he had been reading philosophical texts and Bible commentaries since college. Indeed, he had started reading when he was four and never stopped. He had read, or had been planning to read, virtually every book I mentioned to him, classic or modern.

"But where does the loneliness fit in?" I asked, trying to bring him—and myself—back to his original problem. "What I'm hoping you'll see is that loneliness is not based on the inherent limitations of other people; it is actually an important landmark on the spiritual way, allowing us to separate what is real from what is apparent. In your loneliness, you realize that the question of whether life has meaning is real, while whether the Yankees will win the pennant is not—well, not in the spiritual sense."

By now Eli had recovered fully from his adventure into passion. "Where does the loneliness fit in?" he said, harking back to the beginning of my little sermon. "You're saying that I've used my loneliness to help me separate what's important from what's trivial. I never thought my loneliness was good for anything except making me miserable."

I let his realization echo in the room. Before either of us said anything else, the phone rang. I let it ring. "Aren't you going to answer that?" he asked.

"The machine will pick it up," I said. "I never allow a phone call to interrupt a session. Whatever it is, it can wait." The idea moved him to ruminate:

> That's great. It makes me feel important. I really hate it when I'm talking to someone on the phone and they excuse themselves to answer their call-waiting. I've even had people get back on and say, "I'll have to call you back, there's someone on the other line I have to speak to." Some people are really rude and inconsiderate. Then there are the telemarketers, who somehow know that you've just sat down to dinner.

He was veering off, I thought, into the kind of small talk he so despises in others. "We were talking about separating what was important from what was not," I said as gently as I could.

"Oh, yeah . . . well . . . touché."

I continued, "In addition to separating what is important from what is unimportant, that is, reality from appearance, we also separate other opposite states: left and right, night and day, good and evil. As children, we see these states as so contradictory that we can't imagine that they could be reconciled."

"I know what you mean," Eli said. "I remember how shocked I was the first time I was out in the rain while—impossibly, I thought—at the same time the sun was shining."

But we learn eventually that hardly anything is, or stays, purely one thing or another. Green is a mixture of blue and yellow, night and day are united at dawn and twilight, and there are degrees of good and evil. "Do you see any connection between the sacred and the secular?" I asked.

"I'd love to," he said, "but my acquaintance with the sacred is pretty slim."

I said that I disagreed with him. "We are taught early on that our daily life is secular and that God is sacred. But as we get older, we learn to see the sacred in everyday life: the birds, the sea, the omelet, the painting—all are manifestations of the sacred. In other words, we can use appearance as a gateway to reality."

Here, Eli interrupted me:

> But once we "get it," once we recognize what is truly important, we should be able to see that our neighbors and colleagues are longing for reality as well. I just wish people were less guarded and defensive about their search.

Eli embodied the very contradictions I was trying to illustrate to him in my examples of the ordinary manifestations of the sacred. He could speak easily about the universality of people's search for the sacred and, when pressed, could even describe the loneliness underlying all their brave fronts. But he could not take the next step of actually relating to flesh-and-blood people, whose loneliness was often disguised in small talk. He was, as so many of us are, a strange amalgam of extreme sensitivity and obtuseness. He could describe his own pain with stunning detail and dismiss a colleague's lateness with no curiosity to what might have caused it.

Eli often surprised me by jumping ahead with an insight I hadn't expected from him. I suggested that even if he doesn't find many who would admit to sharing his interest in the meaning of life, in whether we have free will, and the rest, he could find many writings to show him that he was in good company. The moment I said that, he immediately asked for a bibliography, and I was again reminded of how a relationship can, if not carefully tended, turn into an academic one operating only on the cognitive level. So instead of giving him a bibliography, I told him, "Let me introduce you to one who has accompanied me for the past forty years." I handed him the opening pages photocopied from an old translation of Spinoza's *On the Improvement of the Understanding*, in which Spinoza writes, "After experience had taught me that all the usual surroundings of social life are vain and futile; seeing that none of the objects of my fears contained in themselves anything either good or bad, except in so far as the mind is affected by them, I finally resolved to inquire whether there might be some real good. . . ."

I hoped that Eli would follow up on the Spinoza reading I had "assigned" to him, but at our next meeting a month later, I experienced the same disappointment I feel when I've introduced one friend to another and the relationship just doesn't click. He wanted to talk about other things:

> It feels as if ninety percent of virtue is simply to remember. I know what I need to know; I just keep forgetting. Why am I so uncertain each day before I sit down to read and reflect? Why don't I trust the process more? That is what's going on now: I've fallen into radical distrust of the process. I no longer believe there *is* a process, just loneliness, to be followed by more loneliness and growing resentment.

I asked him to explain more about his doubt: had he ever experienced it before? He said that he always experienced it. I noticed him glancing at a fat book that had been sitting on my shelves for so long that I'd forgotten it was there, *The Philosophy of Spinoza*, by a renowned scholar, Harry Austryn Wolfson—the perfect example of the kind of thinking I wanted him *not* to do. I wanted him to get his own experience of Spinoza's philosophy, not Wolfson's and not mine.

"The day after I give up on a book is the day I can finally read past page 2," he remarked.

I was gaining a picture of what the problem was. "It's about control isn't it? Control and surrender."

He responded very softly and, it seemed, remorsefully: "I am still 'playing' at spirituality. To really be spiritual I would have to trust, let go, surrender. But then, who would *I* be?"

Eli was addressing one of the great stumbling blocks for people on the spiritual way: the problem of identity, or individuation. He didn't want to be self-conscious, a trait that lay behind much of his loneliness, but neither was he prepared to let go of the self, a process that frequently poses an obstacle. Was there some other alternative? he asked. I suggested that there wasn't an answer, as if this were some sort of multiple-choice test, but rather, there was a life to live, and if he continued with his reading and his practice, he would see that some of these questions would find their own resolution.

Eli did not return to this quandary directly in our next meeting another month later. Instead he began:

> I will live a rich, full, creative life focused on my values. I must not return to loneliness and the frantic hope of finding community. I must live the life I believe in, and people will emerge, from time to time. On the other hand, perhaps they won't, but I can't let that stop me from doing what I need to be doing.

While I was pleased to hear the energy in his voice, I was also aware of some self-pity in his formulation. Uneasily I asked him, "When you speak of people emerging, what exactly do you mean? It's not as if you live on a desert island. In your daily life you have contact with your immediate family, your extended family, your colleagues at work. These people who 'emerge,' are you assigning some special role to them?"

I looked at the desk in an attempt to give him as much room as he needed. There was a longish pause, but then he continued, as if I hadn't spoken at all.

> I realized long ago that problems are never truly resolved. They recur again and again at different levels of our experience. I thought I had dealt with grieving when my mother died some years back. But then, when my father died, I had to learn grieving all over again. I cannot once and for all overcome hatred, learn to love, be rid of loneliness. I guess that's what you mean when you talk about the ongoingness of time, as you sometimes do—no end of days and no end of the day's tasks.

He isn't going to answer my question, I thought. But his more positive attitude was reflected in what he said next:

> My loneliness is eased not because there are people in my life but because I feel different from others. So much—almost all— depends on me.

That is what I had been trying to convey to him when I had talked to him about the power of naming, but there is nothing like discovering it for yourself. Once again, he appeared to change tacks, but I was beginning to have a better sense of how he appeared to change subjects only to readdress them in his own way.

"A world," he continued,

> that is my first concept. Something that makes you feel you are not alone, that connects you with others, that has shared meanings and values. So first I people my world with the authors of the books I love. Spinoza, thank you, is part of that world. I read

what you gave me and then followed through with the complete text from which the excerpt came and went on to read his *Ethics*. Then I give a visual image of the world in terms of space—not just the comforting space of envelopment, but also the spiritual space I touch when I listen to great music. There is a picture in my Passover Haggadah of a boy with his grandfather. The illustration shows the cozy space of the lit room against the starry night, along with the personal space of the grandfather's enveloping arm around the boy's shoulder. I also sense the larger space of the shared meaning in the Exodus story.

Eli was combining a cognitive world, which comprises meaning and value, and the emotional world of a boy with his grandfather, to arrive at a personal meaning of Passover. It was the first glimpse I got that he could unite the head and the heart. I knew there would be further flashes of this sort before the union became more constant, but for now, I could see that he enjoyed this moment of wholeness. Even his ongoing lament took on a new coloring, as he began to recognize that his dissatisfaction was his own and that he couldn't expect other people to meet his need:

> Once again I am beset by loneliness—the sense that I have no real friends. But I'm learning. Instead of just letting the loneliness sweep over me, I asked myself what I want of people. And the answer is a soul mate. I'm glad I'm getting clearer on that; and now that I know that my "soul mate" can be God, maybe I can lighten the demands I put on people.

I knew from experience that one step forward is all too often followed by two steps backward or even total resistance, so I was delighted when Eli didn't wallow in his loneliness. He went on to question it and saw it as an invitation for greater closeness to God and greater tolerance for people's limitations:

> People aren't there to fill your needs. They are who they are. Occasionally they delight you. But we are all living out our own lives, meeting our own needs, and pursuing our own tasks.

Eli's self-described loneliness was somehow consonant with loving his wife, enjoying his children, being effective in his work. He admitted that people saw him as basically friendly, if somewhat reserved. When he arrived at the concept of "soul mate," he came closer to what he was really trying to express with his sense of loneliness. In junior high school, he couldn't describe the problem—he focused instead on how others saw him. Now he was beginning to realize that the problem lay within himself. His longing was not for some new community—he didn't need to take up a hobby or join a committee. He finally was able to see that his loneliness could not be satisfied by *any* relationship in this world. He was longing for what he came to call the "depth dimension," which underlay and supported all that he perceived.

Eli represented a challenge—even a temptation—for me. I loved the way his mind worked and was tempted to follow up on some of his interesting analogies, but I remembered too well my own experience with a spiritual director when I was first starting out. For a while the relationship had been very helpful, but then we drifted more and more toward academic conversations. The focus, which had been on my relationship to God, shifted to my views about his latest paper. I didn't want to seem ungrateful when he asked me to comment on his academic paper, but I knew that our connection was coming to an end. Now, as I found myself intrigued by some of Eli's formulations, I reminded myself that there was only one focus in our conversations: Eli's relationship to God.

Eli was in unusually good spirits when I saw him a month later. He even looked less harried, less like someone who was courting apoplexy. He had, he said, been playing with numbers—not as a mathematician but in a theological sense. When I expressed my bewilderment he went on:

Early on, we learn that 1 + 1 = 2. Only later do we recognize that 1 + 1 can also equal 1: one drop of water plus one drop of water equals one drop of water—larger, to be sure, but still one drop. So now, when we are trying to come into ever deeper intimacy with God, we are left to wonder if we can do so and still retain any sense of self, or individuality. Will we get absorbed and lost in the oneness of God? In some religious traditions that is the greatest aspiration—overcoming the illusion of individuality. But in Judaism the unique individual self is valued, as God makes room for both our reality and our individuality. This idea fits in with my reflections on loneliness. I don't want to merge in my marriage or in my parenthood. We must love and release.

He paused, pleased with how this had shed some light on his thoughts about loneliness. I told him that while I was impressed with his insights, they were purely cognitive. Where, I wondered, were his emotions?

"We can get back to that," he said, "but I'm not done with the number series—let me continue. Remember, you said at our first session that it's my time to use as I please?"

"My turn to say 'touché,'" I replied, sheepishly.

Anyway, we agree, don't we, that 1 + 1 can equal 1? Now let me show you what I got out of the more common 1 + 1 = 2. I realized how few of us are truly ready to join our oneness (pardon the expression) with another person's. We feel that we are somehow less than one—that is, broken, not whole. And our prospective partner is likewise not fully one. So we ourselves cannot form that wonderful union we dream about, but in trying to form it, we discover that our relationship with God can free us to love, *even in our incompleteness and vulnerability*. Together we can each attain wholeness, so that <1 + <1 = 1 + 1 [less than 1 plus less than 1 equals 1 plus 1]. God is the power that allows us to come into relationship.

This formulation sounded suspiciously like philosopher Martin Buber's words, "God is the eternal Thou behind all our attempts at an I and Thou relationship." I asked whether he had read Buber.

"Yes, of course," he said, but held up his hand. "Not done yet." Before I could say another word, he continued:

> In the miracle of procreation, the union of 1 + 1 brings forth a new 1 that adds to the original 2, giving us the odd-looking equation 1 + 1 = 3. Our child may have one parent's nose and the other's eyes, but this new being is more than a composite of such attributes: it exhibits its own individuality and uniqueness.

"Are you sure you don't have aspirations to become a mathematician?" I interjected, somewhat churlishly.

> Gosh, no! But to go back to the first two 1 + 1's. We think we know that one drop of water plus one drop of water still equals one drop of water, because we think we know what a drop of water is. But water is really a simple description of something that has a lot of hidden potential. A glass of "water" may hold salt in solution, or vinegar, or even cyanide; and it contains, as physicists like to tell us, enough energy to power a nuclear submarine for a year. We don't know our own hidden potential—those traits in ourselves that can come to the fore when our self comes into contact with another. In mathematical terms, 1 (incompletely known self) + 1 equals question mark.

In his own, impersonal way, he was actually getting at something. Anyhow, I realized that I was facing a steamroller, and I could either stand in the middle of the road and get flattened or I could get out of the way. I chose the latter course, partly out of prudence, partly because I was following my own rule, and partly in the knowledge that this vehicle would eventually run out of steam and its driver would run out of breath. But not yet:

Our earliest thinking about our relationship with God takes the form $1 + 1 = 2$: God is 1, I am 1, and together we are 2. This relationship is fully reciprocal, in that I am a character in God's story and God is a character in my story. But if the first 1 is me, the second 1 is another person, and we let $1 + 1 = 2$, then God is not a character in this story but the context in which the story occurs. Put another way, God is the Place of the World. God is not a step in a series but the series itself, which allows the other numbers to come into relationship.

How strange, even overwhelming, that the simplest of problems, $1 + 1$, should yield such complicated answers. But we take for granted the immense symbolic world we enter as children when we can look at our surroundings and learn to apply the word "one" to an apple, a crayon, a wastebasket, a dog, a friend. Our first mathematical lesson provides significant training for us to see the One in and through the diversity of Creation.

Eli finally fell quiet, waiting for my reaction. But he couldn't wait. He burst in again:

"I've got the loneliness thing licked."

"How?" I asked.

"Through the One."

I told him that I admired his work on the One, but that loneliness is not a thought but a feeling. And, if Spinoza was right, then the only thing that can overcome an emotion is a stronger emotion. He smiled, "One is not merely a thought." And he slowly revisited $1 + 1 = 1$; $1 + 1 = 2$; $1 + 1 = 3$; and $1 + x = ?$ with its undisclosed potential. He showed me that each of these points was a discovery. I was impressed.

"You thought all of this was too cognitive," he said,

that I play with numbers to avoid thinking about my family or about my relationship to God. But you can't know how joyous and emotionally engaging this is for me. I realize, not just cognitively but viscerally, that $1 + 1$ is at the heart of my understanding about relationships.

You know that I've read a lot in philosophy. In the early Greek world, there was no real distinction between philosophy on the one hand, and mathematics and science on the other. The number series that we use so blithely to balance our checkbooks was really viewed differently in the Greek world. Numbers were not simply signs or place markers for certain processes; they were real entities with power. As much as I've studied accounting and used numbers the way we all do, I've never lost the sense of excitement and "rightness" I felt when I first read about the early Pythagoreans.

There is power in numbers, and not simply in the way a zero before the decimal point means much more than the same zero after the decimal point. Numbers are a way of talking about reality. Just because people came before us historically doesn't mean they knew less. They knew different things, and they knew them in different ways. My "playing" with $1 + 1 = ?$ is, in part, an attempt to get back to this sense of rightness I had discovered reading early Greek philosophy, but it was also a way of thinking about loneliness itself. Loneliness is my sense that I see, experience, and value this world in a way that is out of sync with the way my contemporaries see it. When I read about the Pythagoreans, I not only understand them, I feel understood. I know that sounds strange, but in their world I feel I am in a context in which other people are looking for ways to express the grandeur and majesty of Creation. I'm suddenly not confined to the twenty-first century, or to my colleagues at work.

So the union of the head and the heart had happened again, and now the flash had lasted longer than a momentary vision.

Eli's work in the banking world had much more to do with reading reports than with meeting people. He said that his younger brother was the sociable one in the family. I pointed out that in all his talking about loneliness, he had not once mentioned his wife. This comment made him uncomfortable, but he answered it. His wife, he said, found community and religion through her synagogue, but that route didn't work for him. He needed to find it on his own, "one on one," he tried to joke. When I displayed only a wan smile but didn't laugh with him, he saw that I was not going to be put off so easily. He reported that he loved his wife but that his loneliness occurred on a different level. They get along well, he said, and shared the same values in raising the children and most everything else, but he didn't want to bore her with his complaints. He thought he now knew that this experience of loneliness was something only he could address. He agreed to note those times when he felt most whole in himself and most free from loneliness. As he left, I suggested that in addition to pondering the one, he might also think about the plus sign.

When I next saw Eli, it was as if someone had played a recording at a faster speed. His actions were faster and more resolute. He walked and spoke more rapidly and more determinedly, and his remarks were more focused. He announced that all was going well, more to dismiss the subject than to explore it. Then he grinned and said, "You really knew what you were asking when you told me to focus on the plus."

I tried to recall our conversation of the previous month, but Eli continued nonstop. He was all but shouting and half out of his seat as he spoke. It was clear that an idea for him was no mere cognitive event. "Holy does not refer to space, as in Holy Land, or to time— Holy Day—holy refers to relationship!"

He looked at me triumphantly, but because I was silent, he realized he couldn't just say "There!" but would have to spell out all the steps leading both to and from his insight.

> You told me to focus on the plus sign. Let me back up a bit. OK, what's a world made up of? Five categories, according to Kant: space, time (these two provide the setting), quantity (that's the 1, 2, 3 business), quality, and relationship. I started with quantity, which is what I'm most familiar with. As I played with the idea of 1 + 1, I realized that I wasn't as familiar with it as I had imagined. It could surprise me. I tried to express some of that surprise the last time we met—I wasn't talking about ideas but about something else coming through, something relational. I

guess you realized that, or you wouldn't have told me to focus on the plus. Once I really looked at the plus, which is relationship, I realized that including it in my thinking affected space and time. Relationship transforms everything. I guess I'd say the plus trumps space, time, and quantity. You asked me when I was most whole, or least lonely, or something like that. Let me tell you that I wasn't lonely for a moment during all the time I was thinking about these things. And not just when I got an idea; sometimes, when I'd just say "1 + 1 = what?" I'd feel—well—different about things.

"You mean quality?" I asked.

"That's *it!* Relationship even trumps quality!"

I let him sit with this idea for a while and then asked, "So what does all this numerology actually mean?"

"You mean, beyond the number system?"

I nodded.

"Well, we agree," he said, "that One is God, or at least *one* of the ones is God—or maybe it's part of the point that we are all ones because we are all in the image of God."

By now he was smiling broadly. "It all works so beautifully. I can say everything I want to say just in terms of 1 + 1 = ?" I continued to sit quietly, and he realized I was waiting for him to finish.

This last point I made, about relationship, I guess that gets at the heart of why I came here in the first place. I love my wife, I love my children, but that doesn't seem to get at the loneliness that's been the underlying motif of my whole life. Maybe it's our shared loneliness, the essential loneliness of the human condition. And as I began to use these symbols, 1 + 1 = ?, it seemed as if it wasn't only me. Not one of us can say, "I am really whole, really one, all by myself." Together we support one another, and together, with God's help, we can become one, whole, and not just individually whole, but we can find reconciliation with those from whom we've been estranged.

Two weeks ago, I had to give a presentation at work. Boy, do I hate doing that! As we were standing outside the conference room, I said—to no one in particular, although Margaret, one of the staffers, was standing there—"Do you ever stop feeling nauseated before you have to make a presentation?" Margaret replied, "Oh, you feel that way too. Don't worry, I'll be there rooting for you." When I glanced her way during the talk, she gave me a thumbs-up sign. Such a small gesture, and yet, when I admitted my vulnerability, what a payoff there was in my feeling of being understood and supported.

I found myself thinking about it later. One direction my thoughts took was the number series again—but another was in terms of vulnerability. I've always thought that it was bad to be vulnerable and one should avoid the feeling at all costs. Yet admitting my fears actually brought me closer to a colleague than a well-formulated presentation. Still later, I tried to bring the two vague feelings together—the one about numbers and the one about vulnerability and my relationship to Margaret. Both seem to suggest that I'm not alone, that I'm part of something larger than myself.

Well, this is embarrassing, but there was still another way that I thought about this. I like to fantasize, but I have a basic rule about my fantasies: they have to be possible. From childhood on I've had a fantasy about being on a desert island—a sort of Robinson Crusoe fantasy, although I did not spend my time trying to get off the island.

I have found that lonely people often choose their loneliness.

In my imagination I made certain that the island was free from predatory beasts and secretly hiding villains. And then I would find or make paper and ink and write. As I grew older I realized that the desert island wouldn't work because it would not have my blood pressure medicine on it. I could no longer be happily stranded because I could no longer survive without the help of medicine. I know this sounds silly, but I felt a real loss when I could not imagine this magnificent retreat. What happened, after my presentation at work, was that I thought again about the island and realized that *I* was the island, I'm the one who has kept everyone at a distance. And the blood pressure medicine, rather than being a handicap, is my liberation. I've always felt that I needed to be self-sufficient, independent, strong. Suddenly I can see that my imagined strength was my weakness, that vulnerability—maybe call it humanity—is freeing. I am not on an island but part of an archipelago. I'm part of something much larger than this isolated island, and this something larger is—this sounds so audacious—God.

Whether I think about the number series, or my island, or the incident at work, I'm trying to say that the One, that is, God, is really behind, in, and through every relationship. And I don't mean this is something I think, but this is something I feel. I'm not accustomed to saying I feel or experience God.

"Why are you so uncomfortable?"

That's a fair question. I feel like a little kid who claims to know something he has no business knowing. Wait, I know where that comes from. I was a little kid, and I had been going to Sunday school—it was years before my bar mitzvah. I used to like to get to Sunday school early and slip into the sanctuary. There would be no lights on except the eternal light in front of the ark, illuminating the curtain behind which stood the Torahs. I felt something there, in the dark, but I also thought I'd better not tell anyone about it. I knew even then that the Jewish experience of God was never 1 + 1 but was always the Jewish people + 1.

"Wait—" I commented, "how many people crowded around Abraham when he recognized that God was One? And where were the slew of witnesses when Jacob wrestled with God? But we don't have to stay with biblical figures. You tell me you've read Buber and Heschel, and you've worked with the Spinoza text. Each of these people, regardless of how many others they subsequently influenced, also had to think through their own thoughts and enter into the mystery of their own loneliness to draw out a great gift."

Eli was silent, but in a new way. He was genuinely thinking about what I had said and not rushing to defend his own position.

> I'm so embarrassed. I'm the person who told you that Jews are not comfortable with 1 + 1 = 1, that our individuality and uniqueness are valued and must be preserved. I know that we mustn't lose ourselves in community, and I don't always know what I know. I love the new community you've put me in: Abraham, Jacob, Spinoza, Buber, and Heschel.

Over the ensuing months, Eli not only recognized his relationship with Abraham, Jacob, Spinoza, Buber, and Heschel, he also, finally, got a sense of Judaism's larger context and his role in it—not merely to take from it but also to contribute to it. He understood that *his* experience of God and *his* deepening one-on-one relationship with God will be infused back into Judaism to strengthen others.

6

PAUL

A Philosopher on His Deathbed Reexamines His Work

I met Paul some thirty-five years ago at the first faculty meeting I attended at the college where I had just begun to teach. He sat down next to me and introduced himself as an elder statesman at the college. I had heard of him—he had a national reputation—and I even had one of his half-dozen books on my shelf of publications I planned to read someday but not now. He was pleased to learn that I was teaching philosophy. I must admit that we continued our conversation throughout much of the meeting, which dealt at length with some trivial matters I no longer recall—perhaps because I wasn't devoting my full attention to the discussion. After some initial sparring over the relative merits of Plato and Aristotle, we became good friends, and he turned out to be something of a mentor for me during my own first years of teaching.

I respected him deeply, as did the students, who flocked to take his classes. When I saw that he was slated to teach Literature of the Bible, I obtained his permission to audit the course. I was, of course, keenly interested in the content, but I was just as fascinated by how he organized the material, challenged his students, and explained the more obscure distinctions. I witnessed firsthand the great respect with which he treated the class and saw, to my surprise, that no student was ever embarrassed to speak up in the presence of this well-known scholar. Regardless of how misworded, or even misguided, a student's question might be, Paul considered it thoughtfully and then used it to bring out further insights from the text. He treated every comment and every interruption as a gift.

In the following ten years, I was privileged to sit in on more of his classes. Then, for another four years after he retired, he continued seeing students who were doing independent-study projects with him or writing theses under his tutelage. He would meet them at the college, where he came regularly to work on his next book. But eventually, he was diagnosed with Parkinson's disease, and finally, walking and some of the other tasks of daily life became too difficult for him to continue coming in. Although we had spoken on the phone a few times, I had not seen him for about a year when his wife, Vera, told me that he was declining. She let me know that he was hospitalized with what might be his final illness. I was eager to visit Paul because I loved him and wanted to let him know how much having him as a colleague and a friend had meant to me. I hadn't realized that he might also have a reason for wanting to see me.

Paul's door was open, and he welcomed me weakly but warmly. He put down the book he was reading, W. Gunther Plaut's *The Torah: A Modern Commentary*, which had recently been published. He looked very pale, and for the first time I noticed how wrinkled his face was and how old he appeared, especially sitting up in bed in his pajamas instead of pacing around, excited and nattily dressed, in front of a classroom. When he told me after the briefest of pleasantries that he wanted to discuss "final questions" with me, I felt unprepared, even shocked. I reminded myself that I was never prepared, but that if I could get myself quiet and centered, I could hope to be guided. Trying to guide someone spiritually is an awesome prospect, and never more so than when the guidee is a former mentor on his deathbed, because there is no time for you to correct your mistakes. I silently prayed while Paul sent Vera out of the room. She had been at his bedside constantly since early morning and looked haggard but stoic. I then asked Paul to tell me what was on his mind.

He said:

> As I am lying here on my deathbed—no, don't protest, I haven't
> suddenly become stupid—I thought of the books I've written.
> I keep asking myself what I have accomplished through my
> writing.

Together we drew out the beginning of an answer. Paul was a
Jewish rationalist who had attacked superstition and fought unending
battles with people who were trapped in rigid modes of thought. He
had given new meaning to revelation and shown that rationality
could be a route to the holy. But was that really enough? he wondered. Also, he judged that few people could travel with him the
entire route he had mapped out so painstakingly in his works. Of all
the generations of students he had taught, how many truly understood what was at stake in his last book?

Paul declared that he really lacked nothing. He had fellowship if
he wanted it, but he didn't crave it. He had food enough—it was even
kosher, he said—but he rarely thought about it. He had worlds of
ideas that called to him each morning, promising a day of refreshing
mental exercise. One of the fictions Paul used to amuse himself was
to imagine a heavenly banquet, a practice dating to rabbinic times, at
least. But instead of Abraham, Isaac, Jacob, Moses, Joshua, and David,
Paul's banquet hall was crowded with Y'hudah HaLevi, Ibn Ezra,
Maimonides, Gersonides, Descartes, Aristotle—then he paused as he
drew up the list: "Should Socrates and Plato be included?" he said,
humorously recalling our intermittent bantering over the relative
merits of Plato and Aristotle. Paul invoked Plato's *Symposium*, a celebration of beauty. He then announced that were he to live, he would
write a new book, on beauty. He had already shared with the world
his thoughts on how to live and on what constitutes the good life.

> It isn't fair that Aristotle is considered a dry philosopher,
> because we have none of his own writing, just notes taken by his
> students. No wonder he doesn't have the carefully constructed

images we find in Plato. Even so, an occasional poetic line managed to creep into his work, such as the famous saying "One swallow does not make a summer."

Suddenly, Paul began coughing and choking. I rushed over to the head of the bed, but he raised his hand to hold me in place. He quieted down, spit into a cloth near his pillow, and then continued as if the incident hadn't occurred. Medical questions aside, Paul said he still had a problem. Plato records Socrates as saying that he had written some verses earlier on his final day. Paul had never written a poem, or even told a story to a niece or nephew. In Plato's *Phaedo*, which Paul had recently reread, Socrates speaks of philosophy as a form of art. Paul, like Socrates, had always associated art with artifice and rejected the arts as untrue. So his rereading of Socrates' decision to write poetry on the final day of the philosopher's life would have caused Paul to sit up, "had I not been too weak." Instead, he allowed himself to think of the two artists he most loved: Vermeer, who taught him something about light and space, and Rembrandt, whose self-portraits continued to inspire him. Neither had painted decorative pictures. Rembrandt's self-portraits weren't pretty, he noted, but they were beautiful. The recollection of Rembrandt's drawings and etchings troubled him. He returned to Socrates' reassuring statement that philosophy was the greatest art form.

Paul's own writing, although sparse and even severe, contains a whole world overflowing with the fullness of life. In his books, he evokes the streets of his native Chicago, the light on the pavement in the early morning, the sounds and the smells, all as examples of various scholarly points. Even lately, in the semi-seclusion of his study and now of his hospital room, the color and cacophony of the bustling city remained in his consciousness. Beauty was all around him—everywhere but in his major work. His recollections of the city brought tears to his eyes. Was recalling his native city indulging in imagination? But is imagination necessarily false? He haltingly quoted Wallace Stevens's statement that "reality is an activity of the most august imagination." I couldn't tell if his hesitancy was due to

his illness or to the frightening thought that he may have under-
valued imagination.

When a nurse came in to check Paul's vital signs, I moved to Vera's
chair. I was afraid he would lose his train of thought, but he kept right
on talking even as she checked his catheter bag, waited for the ther-
mometer to beep, and took his pulse. She turned to me and told me
not to tire him out, as he winked behind her back. After she left, he
started coughing again but quieted down more quickly than last time,
and he continued:

> Plato's description of Socrates' death gives expression to my own
> sense of dying—at peace, but still caring about the same essential
> questions. But one difference is that Socrates speaks of creativity
> and of philosophy as art forms, and he speaks of beauty, and I
> never did; probably graduate school beat the idea out of me.

I started to remind him of how he had led generations of students
to love the novels and dramas he taught, but he allowed no praise or
soothing words. With a ferocity I had never seen before, he continued, "What if, while seeking to guide people, I led them astray?" With
his eyes half shut, he asked for my view of Plato's position on beauty.
Plato did not fall prey to the popular notions of beauty and ugliness,
I said, or good and evil that Paul had always taken pains to refute.
What had Socrates learned in his foray into poetry? Paul could not
enter into Socrates' mind, but he forced himself to recall his own
vision of Rembrandt's self-portrait. What had he seen there?

He concluded that what had taken him eight books to express
comes across just as well in the brushstrokes of the painting. The
beauty of the self-portrait had engaged him—he had felt connected
to the aging painter, looking into the eyes that had seen so much
anguish without betraying any bitterness. He had tried to structure
his own philosophical system so that it would engage the reader, not
be passively assimilated.

From somewhere unknown to me, I began a response: "The philosophical life is still first and foremost a life, so it contains all the

events of life: working, eating, doing what is called for, suffering what has to be borne. What makes it more than a life is our relationship to God in and through all that happens to us. Just as Vermeer's style persists regardless of what subject he painted, so God's presence can be perceived regardless of the events and the contexts. So, perceiving God becomes the ultimate way to view life. In a way it's like the ground bass that is repeated over and over in, say, an aria by Henry Purcell, that 'grounds' the piece while the singer may sing of love, joy, terror, or death. The bass persists unchanged throughout the piece and serves as the 'base' (same root) supporting all the notes above.

"Beauty entails seeing all of life as a blessing: recognizing our good experiences as blessings—that's the easy part—but also forging blessings out of pain and suffering and tragedy and loss. Beauty needs to be made and remade."

We moved on to discuss Ecclesiastes, which Paul described as a starting point for him. Paul had focused on the phrase "Vanity of vanities, all is vanity," but I reminded him of another line, "He makes everything beautiful in its time and puts eternity into man's mind so he cannot find out what God has done from beginning to end." I told Paul that to my mind, this verse equates beauty with fittingness, as Socrates also did. But it also tells us that reason has limits. Pushed far enough, reason reaches a boundary, and that is where I believe beauty has a role to play. The existence of music and poetry, the qualities of beauty and rhythm—why do they have the capacity to catch us up in wonder, and why do they exist? Somehow the beautiful informs us about levels of reality that are otherwise closed to us. In the presence of beauty, the world seems charged with a new vitality, with a splendor that doesn't belong to it but pours through it, as light pours through a stained-glass window.

Paul quoted to me a line he had read: "The beautifier—not the beautified—is beautiful." Then he said:

When I look at something beautiful, of course I see it, but I see something beyond it—maybe its maker, maybe something about a harmony or fittingness. It is never just about itself, it opens us to something more.

Beauty can evoke what many philosophers have taken pains to map. Beauty not only can reconcile opposites, it can also bring us to knowledge. I remember the first time I saw a work of modern art that deliberately juxtaposed clashing colors: the more I stared at it—and it really did feel as though it hurt my eyes—the more I saw that the warring colors really opened up the painting to a larger resolution, and that was beauty. For Paul, the idea that beauty could bring people to the same insights that his philosophy had pointed to was both exciting and somewhat frightening.

Here Paul stopped abruptly and asked me to get the nurse. I hurried to the nurses' station, stopping on the way to tell Vera that he had asked for a nurse. She sighed and said, "He's probably embarrassed with you there to ask that his catheter be adjusted."

She went into the room with the nurse while I stayed outside. After less than five minutes, the nurse left, and Vera told me that Paul wanted her back out and me back in. He looked unchanged, and he picked up the conversation as if I had never left. He recalled the breakthrough he experienced when he struggled with writing *The Rationalists in Confrontation*. He had experienced a gift of knowing that came to him after hours of staring at the sunlight playing off a blank page he was trying to fill. Experientially he had known, though he had not stated it clearly in his philosophy, that the highest form of knowledge comes to us as a gift: like the ability to ride a bicycle or work a clutch, it comes as a sudden illumination, a stroke of genius, true contemplation.

"Have I misled the people I sought to help?" he asked. "I've praised reason in a book written with the help of an intuitive gift."

No, I assured him, he had been right in warning that insight requires great effort—but the effort doesn't cause the knowledge, it's just a precondition for it. We have to prepare the ground, but the plants bloom by themselves.

And on this, perhaps his final day, he returned to the phrase from Ecclesiastes, the source of his greatest torment and the source of the verse that had fueled his whole adult life, "Vanity of vanities . . ." Ecclesiastes expresses the despair of one man who refuses to be himself.

Paul was whispering now, saying something I had heard him say in different forms over the years: that part of Plato's accepting himself and his work lies in his statement that philosophy is a great art form. Paul agreed that it was but said that that did not assuage his own guilt about failing to discuss beauty in any of his books. But in this time outside of time, he chose to reconcile himself to this lack. His chief defense, he thought, was that he so prominently discusses love. And what, I asked him, is the relationship of beauty to love?

He closed his eyes again, and I thought he had fallen asleep, but he called out to me to get Vera. I started moving toward the door to leave, but Vera assured me that they had had many hours to talk and she thought he still had more to say to me. And then he quoted by heart from one of Socrates' final speeches:

> "I thought it would be safer not to take my departure before I had cleared my conscience by writing poetry and so obeying the dream. I began with some verses in honor of the god whose festival it was. When I had finished my hymn, I reflected that a poet, if he is to be worthy of the name, ought to work on imaginative themes, not just descriptive ones, and I was not good at inventing stories. So I availed myself of some of Aesop's fables, which were ready to hand and familiar to me, and I versified the first of them that suggested themselves."
>
> Here was Socrates, who had lived his entire life distinguishing reality from appearance and had even offered a stern critique of art as imitation. Yet, on his last day on earth, he wrote verses without embarrassment or regret, proving that he saw art and beauty as real after all.

With his eyes still closed, Paul asked in a whisper, "Is it too late for me to pay my debt to beauty?"

I told him that he had already offered an exquisite gift of beauty in his books, which allow the perceptive reader to see everything in its relationship to God, or in Goethe's words, "God's presence in each element."

And with his wife holding his hand, he uttered what turned out to be his final words before he lost consciousness: "I love you—the world is beautiful."

7

FLORENCE

Understanding the Creative Process

Florence was a dedicated high school English teacher whose teaching of literature always made students struggle with questions about the meaning of their lives and what they were trying to become. She had already decided at fourteen that she wanted to teach children and write poetry that conveyed her ideas. She was forceful in her thinking and her arguments, and also formidable in appearance. She had a keen sense of fairness and tried to learn how to fight for justice without being consumed by anger.

Florence showed up in my office during an exceptionally cool spell in August, when a slight nip in the air gave a portent of the fall that would soon follow. She wore a herringbone tweed jacket over a white blouse that was closed at the throat with a large brooch. Her solid brown skirt was uncompromisingly straight, her brown Oxfords served as the foundation for a deliberate no-nonsense look. She was around five foot seven and weighed at least 250 pounds. I could imagine her students filing into her classroom for the first time and almost cowering in her presence. I made a hasty judgment (which turned out to be an oversimplification) that she must be uncomfortable lugging around all that weight.

Florence reported to me that she had lost her home. I expressed both shock and bewilderment. She then explained:

I am speaking metaphorically. What has happened is that the Ritual Committee in my synagogue has voted to change prayer books, so that my house of worship no longer feels like home.

Many people get annoyed when their language of prayer is altered or a favorite hymn is discarded, but Florence was talking about much more than annoyance. She told me how language has always played a central role in her life. She said that she taught literature and wrote poetry. She had one daughter, a teenager, who learned to talk before she learned how to walk, and who learned to read at such an early age that she doesn't even remember not being able to read. Her husband was a speechwriter for a political action group. She went on to explain what she thought was the origin of her profound commitment to language:

When I was nine years old, I was poling a rowboat along the swampy far shore of a lake. The rowboat was so close to the shore that the top of the oar that I used for poling frequently hit the overhanging tree limbs. Suddenly I banged my head into one of the branches and was thrust into prelinguistic time. Only gradually could my brain inform me that I had dislodged a snake from the branch and it now sat in the bottom of my boat. Thirty years later I can still feel my inability to recall the word "snake" and all that went with it, such as an awareness of possible danger or the capacity to wonder what to do. All I can remember, though not express, is what the tumble into languagelessness felt like. Language and thought processes returned when I became conscious of the snake's presence. I could gauge the length of the oar and consider the possibility of sliding the oar under the snake and lifting it out of the boat. Long after I pushed off, snakeless, from the shallows and was safely back in the deep of the lake, the uncanniness of that temporary aphasia stayed with me. Language had not only restored the snake to my world, it had also reawakened my capacity to deal with it. In retrospect, although it was probably fright that robbed me of words, the loss of language was more terrifying than the presence of the intruder. I could not communicate with myself. Had I merely lost the word "snake," I could have thought around it—squiggly large worm. But I had lost all language, and only when I regained it could I understand the concepts snake, boat, and oar.

Her experience with language connected her with the biblical notion that God created the world by word alone, "And God said . . ." This recognition was both cognitive and visceral, and it was personally confirmed by her snake experience, in which her world came into being through language. The same recognition was a major factor in her choice of study, and her increasing linguistic sophistication helped her separate ideas from mere verbiage. For example, in discussing curriculum at her school, administrators were always looking to rename programs rather than actually change them. Her concern with language also translated into an abhorrence of inauthenticity, including the all-too-prevalent refusal to call things by their right names. Students with long disciplinary records, who used to be called simply "bad," were now referred to as "challenging." Every year, she confided, she was assigned a class of such "challenging" students. Though told that she was given these classes because she had a special gift for handling them, the real reason, she knew, was that she herself was always "challenging" the principal of the school, especially on issues of equity and justice for students. Her most recent argument with the principal centered on the lack of financial support for the string quartet—they needed good music stands—while the school paid thousands for keeping the football team in uniforms and Gatorade.

I was interested in her opening remark about having lost her home. Because Florence used language so precisely, I asked her to explore this notion of "home" further. What did it mean to her? She contrasted the old and new liturgies by comparing them to a Shakespeare play versus a review-notes version of the play, which provides the plot without the poetry. She also said that what to her had been a stately home with wood paneling and careful architectural details had been replaced by a characterless, poured-concrete development house that would shelter her from wind and rain but bring no sense of comfort or beauty.

When we met again, in September, I had had a month in which to mull over her situation. She had told me at our first meeting that she was on a full-year sabbatical and wanted to take the time seriously, to rethink her values and recommit to her teaching and her religion. I suggested that she emerge from the inadequate shelter she had described and face the wind and rain—that is, replace what she saw as the insipid language of the new liturgy with the chaos and potential richness of silence. I knew that most people are afraid of pure silence, that breathtakingly empty space that demands to be filled. But Florence had special reason to be afraid, given that her childhood experience of silence—losing speech in the presence of the snake—became a cause for terror. My suggestion that she enter into silence was deliberate, and I wanted to be sure that Florence knew why I thought that the experience would be important for her, so I said: "Silence precedes speech and gives rise to it. The Jewish mystics suggest that the world is sustained by people's capacity to hold their tongue. This idea is expressed in a commentary on a line in the Book of Job, 'God suspends the world on nothing,' which is taken to mean that 'God suspends the world on our capacity for silence.'" This interpretation intrigued Florence. I was tempted to offer other mystical texts, but Florence cut me short: "No more talk; experience."

When I next saw Florence, leaves were crunching underfoot, and fall was in full swing. She informed me that she was planning a "fast" beginning on Rosh HaShanah and ending on Yom Kippur—a fast from language. I suggested that she might like to start with one day rather than ten, but she felt it was a form of penance for the fury she had been feeling during most of the services she had attended in the past month. She said, without a hint of irony, that these Ten Days of Penitence were the right time for this undertaking. How, I asked, would she accomplish her goal, with a husband and a teenager at home?

My daughter asked if I could really go for a week without criticizing her. My husband was wonderfully supportive when I told him, volunteering to dispose of phone calls and do the shopping.

She would not talk, naturally, but she would also not listen to the radio, watch television, or read anything. We agreed to meet the week after Yom Kippur to discuss what she had learned and how it had affected her view of the Yom Kippur liturgy.

I may well have been more eager to see her than she was to see me after the holidays. How had she managed the week? I wondered. She began by reporting that she had "cheated" a little, admitting that she had made a few notes. She supposed that real silence would have meant not only not taking in any noise but also not producing any. I reminded her that the twentieth-century Trappist monk Thomas Merton had managed to write more than fifty books after taking a vow of perpetual silence. She decided that her telegraphic notes still left her, for the most part, in silence. She read me single phrases and sentences, and seeing that some context was needed, she elaborated after each one.

"Crowding out this blessed time with busyness." I realized that much of the noise was internally produced—I was the one who was distracting myself. I didn't simply write that I crowded out this time with busyness, but that I crowded out this *blessed* time with busyness, that is, I experienced something holy.

"Silence is wonder, abiding mystery, nondomesticated, untamed." I was terrified. Not the terror I experienced with the snake, but a terror of approaching the Holy of Holies. I knew there would be riches there if I could only allow myself to fully enter the silence.

"I am now aware of all the noises in my daily life, and I can briefly shut them out. When I do, I experience a deep stillness."

As if on cue, a car alarm went off outside. We both chuckled, and she continued:

I meant both the external noises, such as the traffic constantly whirring in the background (and, yes, the car alarms), the refrigerator humming, the clock ticking; and the internal ones—worrying about unanswered e-mail, wondering what my daughter is doing, thinking about the errands I have to run. The stillness I felt was more than silence, deeper than the absence of noise. It was powerful enough to make me feel I could be genuinely at home in it. But the most important thing about it was that the silence allowed me to see ways in which I needed to change. I know that change is difficult—it means letting go of something familiar and taking a chance on something new.

She did not elaborate on the types of change she was seeking but continued reading her notes:

"Silence—the silence of God? The silence of God is the silence of my creativity. Silence without inspiration." It wasn't always wonderful. When I wrote this, I was feeling silence as a void, not a plenum, that the silence was *against* me. I was waiting to hear a voice, but there was none to be heard, staying in expectation but feeling abandoned. But my negative feelings about silence would change a few hours later, as mysteriously as they had come.

"Silence/solitude/darkness—in which I see lights. Embarking on an adventure." That was the opposite pole of my creative lack. Now I felt that there was a whole rich domain for me to explore and that I was beginning to do so. I felt I was setting out on a great journey. How much uncharted territory there is within, enough for me to explore for the rest of my life. I left my intentional period of silence with a deep resolve to cultivate silence and simplicity, but I still had to face the Yom Kippur services. I was very uneasy going to services. I didn't want to greet my fellow worshipers or enter into chitchat. Fortunately, my introspective attitude was entirely appropriate for the day, and no one tried to engage me in conversation. As I read from the prayer book, I found the silence again, all around the edges of the prayers, and realized that my prayer led to silence. As the day waned, I felt the silence growing. My experience of silence had helped me to perceive it under, around, and through all of the services.

And then the poet and English teacher shone through:

I guess genuine prayer brings you to silence in just the way poetry draws you to the whiteness of the page. As John Keats wrote, "Heard melodies are sweet, but those unheard / Are sweeter."

Over the next few months, Florence complained, again, both about services and about the community in her synagogue. She began her complaints by returning to her earlier frustration with the language of the prayer book. I reminded her that language is like religion in that both need community to have meaning. Her frown and her silence suggested I was touching on something close to the area of the problem. Florence was discovering that her difficulties with prayer lay much deeper than the changes in language she found in the prayer book.

It was urgent for Florence to distinguish between communal prayer and her own private prayer. I suggested that prayer required us to assert the truth, even our frustrations and inadequacies. All genuine relationships require honesty at their base, and a relationship with God demands no less. It is scary to admit that you are frightened or that you are wavering in belief, or that you sought greater intimacy but are now having second thoughts. Florence said that she was learning to be honest about herself but that doing so made her dislike herself ("I'm such a whiner," she declared). But realizing that she disliked herself finally gave her the chance to see what changes she would have to make.

You know how I love language. You even know that I've written many academic papers. What I haven't shared is that I now take my writing to be my major concern. But that is a problem. Creativity and religion seem to point in opposite directions. Religion points to authority and obedience, while creativity points to an inner authority and not playing by the rules.

"But religion," I said, "as experienced by the Psalmist, was not secondhand and still allowed for creativity and religion to coexist."

Florence asked, "So where does tradition come in?"

I held that tradition gives us the domain, but then we go beyond that domain to create something new. If Emily Dickinson hadn't begun from an acceptance of rhyme, her strange inner rhymes and assonances would not have pushed the poetic limits of her time into something breathtakingly new. Religion transmits the insights of its greatest thinkers, formulated in the expression of their time and culture. We accept what was given, but we have to remake it to fit our own time and to express our own unique experiences.

Finally, in the depth of winter, the day came when Florence recognized that the problem was not the change in the worship service or even a fascination with prayer. As she put it:

> What I was struggling with all along is the conflict between the poet and the mystic. Sometimes I see the two as identical—the mystic giving us the vision, while the poet gives us words, which I take as giving reality to the vision. But sometimes I return to the earlier meaning of poetry—from the Greek *poesis*—"maker," or "doer." Then I sense a tension between the two. The poet is maker, master, fabricator, while the mystic is the receiver, lover, servant of God.

Here Florence returned to her experience of Yom Kippur: "Yom Kippur is a call to become as good at being ourselves as we can be."

"But," I chimed in, "it also provides us ways to *not hear* the call. We can easily focus on fasting and the hunger it produces, rather than on the idea it is supposed to provoke—that everything we have is a gift from God. We can concentrate our energy on making sure that the prayers are said correctly, rather than on the transformation to which they call us."

Florence eagerly picked up the theme:

> Yes, we can pay attention to preparing for the holy day, rather than preparing ourselves to live a life of awareness of, and openness to, serving God. If we think only about our "sins," we might feel we're not *that* bad. But life is a precious gift, and we are surely not called upon to be mediocre—"not that bad"; rather, we are called to be brilliant at being ourselves. No comparisons with others are relevant. Judaism once had a fervor for living— when did we let it get calmed, tamed? When did conforming with others overtake conforming to God?

Where did these thoughts come from? Clearly those ten days from Rosh HaShanah through Yom Kippur had stirred up some profound thinking. For starters, I said that conforming never seemed to be her problem, that she was very much her own woman. Yes, she agreed, but it represented one way that she felt less in common with other members of her congregation. As to the rest of her ideas, it was clear that her discomfort had become the occasion for her to enter into stillness, and in the process, other issues came to the fore:

> I have worked at breaking the surface of deadness and triviality to get over my childhood feeling that "life is but a dream." I've always found it strange that everyone can blithely sing "Row, row, row, your boat, gently down the stream, / Merrily, merrily, merrily, merrily, *life is but a dream*," without getting caught on those words.

She actually sang the whole verse, forcefully emphasizing the last five words.

> At first, that phrase caused a distinct feeling of disappointment to come over me, especially when something I had longed for

came true, because it never lived up to my expectations. Later, I came to feel that life is but an *empty* dream. I would counter the feeling by some physical action, usually drinking water and swallowing hard. That would restore me to the present. But the problem lay there, and I finally had to address it head-on.

What does "life is but a dream" really signify? Many existentialists would say not that life is a dream, but that our belief in its meaningfulness is a dream or, as psychologists put it, an illusion. I knew that Florence did not believe that, but had she in her childhood? We talked about classmates in school who thought one view was just as good as another, as opposed to her own firm rooting in absolute values and in a designed and purposeful universe. She had no use for cynicism and nihilism. She still recalled her sense that her fellow graduate students who were convinced that life was meaningless were no more sophisticated than she was. What made them think that, just because they had accepted a negative view, they were superior? She personally was on the side of life and hope and meaning.

Moving beyond her beloved English texts, I referred Florence to *Pirkei Avot*, a talmudic text called "The Ethics of the Fathers." We find there a list of what to bring to your study, and it includes "being beloved," which means that we must think about those who love us. I told her that we were here now only because certain people nourished and sustained us with love, and reclaiming them would of course be a good thing. But "being beloved" means even more, because we are also loved by God, and with that recognition our reading of texts becomes transformed. If you read a text in order to find out what God wants you to discover there, your whole approach is different.

Florence was immediately intrigued by the idea. She spoke about how she herself introduces students to texts and how she imagines that there is a growing relationship between the student and the author—dare she say love? Occasionally, especially in her senior honors classes, some students have come to regard authors as old friends. If she could bring them that far in just a few years of high school, how far could the Rabbis bring the Jewish people over generations of study of the sacred texts?

Obviously something had been triggered during Florence's ten days, and the process had not stopped. She was no longer referring back to those days; instead, she was bringing a whole new approach to her field of literature. She had always been a thoughtful reader of texts and an engaging teacher as well. But now she was challenging herself to unite her new spiritual insights with her teaching commitments. Each time I saw her, I found new evidence of a process that was taking on a life of its own, as when she said:

> We cannot learn to walk without falling, or play a piece of music without hitting a wrong note. We cannot avoid the falls or wrong notes, but we *can* learn from them and get on with the job. We must put aside judgment, beginning with judging ourselves. I must be gentle with myself and equally gentle with others. In the realm of spirituality, we are all either beginning or convalescing, and we need encouragement, tolerance, and support.

I was amazed to hear this teacher, who had a reputation for being fair but tough, expound on the virtues of encouragement and support. Then she took yet another tack:

> The idea of destiny intrigues me. I am needed! There is something that I uniquely can contribute to this world. And in those moments when I focus on what I uniquely can contribute, I am most free. Those days of silence were about finding my unique destiny, and thereby finding my freedom and joy.

I wanted her to get at what she really meant by her new interest in destiny. Was she thinking of not teaching? She dismissed my question, saying that she needed to wait—to get quiet, still, and open—before she could understand where her thoughts were going. And the waiting itself had become a place, not simply a way station. I knew what she meant when she alluded to this spatial conception of time. I had felt it myself some years earlier and tried to recall whether I had ever told Florence about that experience. But my major responsibility and obligation were to listen to what she told me. Most of the transformation that she was undergoing had a momentum of its own, so for the next few months, as winter gradually left New York and spring took up residence, I encouraged her ongoing insights.

Florence was beginning to realize that only when we approach the world, not to study or categorize it but to relate to it, can we rejoice. The "studying" mode estranges us. It is through relationship that we come to know, come to be expanded, but that is what joy is, according to Spinoza's definition: moving from a lesser to a greater perfection. It was hard for Florence, a confirmed cognitive type who has always been rewarded for studying, analyzing, and deconstructing, to recognize how much all her education and training had taken her away from what was natural and joyous. But clearly, she was moving away from her "received" way of thinking and teaching, though not away from teaching and writing. Her new approach was bringing a fresh perspective to the way she interacted with the world.

Did you ever wonder how I became so—obese? I'm not uncomfortable talking to you about it. Believe it or not, I learned through a year of therapy that while it was not a conscious decision, there was an element of choice involved. I wanted, above all, to be taken seriously. You might say that I took the metaphor "weighty" or "having stature" too literally. You know how women were regarded in my day—heck, the way they are still regarded today: they can be cute or ugly, libidinous or ice queens, that is, they are judged mostly by how attractive or how available they are. The only way to have my poetry appraised objectively was to step outside those categories and be, in effect, sexless. (Fortunately, my size didn't stop my dear husband from falling in love with me—the intellectual, nonphysical me, to be sure.) It was a high price to pay, but I paid it. I used to sign my poems with initials instead of my first name, to make it look as though I were male. But I don't have to tell you—you certainly lived through those bad old days.

What I've done to myself in teaching and writing I seem to be repeating in religion. All of this began many years ago, but now it has to stop. Last month I had a bad physical: my doctor told me to shape up or I would have to face adult-onset diabetes. He scared me, but he also made me realize that I can't be serious about opening to God and not address the ways I have cut myself off from my own physical being. This is all very frightening, but God seems to be calling me in every possible direction. I actually bought myself a new piece of clothing. Once a group of department chairwomen at my school met for coffee, and we noticed that not one of us was wearing pink. We had deliberately avoided pink in order not to fulfill "their" stereotypes. Well, what I bought is not exactly pink, but it is a soft rose color. Probably the only person who will see me wearing it is my husband, but it's a start.

Although I doubted very much that she had deliberately made herself fat for whatever reasons, I let the thought go, having neither the desire nor the skill to take on what I judged to be a psychological issue. I did, however, ask her what she meant by her statement that what she had done to herself in teaching she seemed to be repeating in religion.

She answered immediately:

I restricted the ways in which God could approach me. I allowed myself to be unattractive. I couldn't allow God to love me, because love has been so tainted by sexism. But—

And she paused. I repeated her "But—" with a questioning rise in my voice.

I think I'm ready to use the gifts of my feminine insight in my classroom and maybe also in Judaism. Although I must say that it feels strange to be so Jewish when Judaism has so little use for women.

"If not Judaism, then what?" I asked.

She mentally flailed around looking for a nonpatriarchal religion, dismissing neo-paganism as too new for her classical bent and altogether lacking in magnificent texts. Then, in a more reflective mood, she said, "As flawed and sexist as the transmission has been, Judaism has been my way to God. But how can I smash the idols of patriarchy?"

"Bring forward the women," I volunteered.

What she said next was close to something that I'd often said myself:

> There are texts in the Torah that I dislike intensely, but I still find them to be overall nourishing and formative. In the same way, there are aspects of teaching high school that I dislike almost as much. But—and it's a key "but"—teaching is a context that brings together my deepest loves: trying to serve God, working with youngsters, teaching material I really care about, and having the chance to learn more and to write. Probably every profession has its good and bad points, so my motto is "Accept it and move on."

Over our next two meetings, I couldn't help but notice that Florence's face was taking on more definition, as if her cheeks had been the first to feel the effects of her dieting. Almost shyly, she announced that her daughter had just given her a birthday present. She reached into her briefcase and removed a small velvet bag. Slowly she drew out a compact of blush, a small eye shadow, a light lipstick, and a spray cologne.

> She noticed, and she's supporting my changes. It all began with my trying to be open to God and then trying to care for the gift of life that God had given me, and in the process, I wind up drawing closer to my husband and daughter.

Florence paused, and for the first time since I had known her, she was speechless. After a period of quiet, she began again:

> In my desire to be a serious person, a teacher, a writer, I deformed part of myself. It took a health scare to finally get me to see it, but in the process I was given so much more than a chance to regain my health. I was given a chance to reclaim my wholeness. Part of me could feel chided by my daughter's birthday present, but I don't—I feel supported. Part of me could bewail all those years that I disowned my [here she actually blushed] femininity.
>
> Femininity is not a bad thing, it is an undervalued thing. I have always taken pride in being able to think for myself, that is, not running with the crowd. It's embarrassing to see how much I internalized society's denigration of the feminine: I went along with everyone else and made fun of intuition by calling it "women's intuition." The feminine carries gifts that I need to reclaim. Women aren't better than men, nor are they any less than men; they are equally human. I took comfort in the Torah's depiction of the major characters.

Together we looked through the Torah, with its honest assessment of the flaws in our ancestors. The men are certainly flawed—Abraham in his banishment of Hagar and Ishmael to the desert, Jacob in stealing his father's blessing from Esau, Joseph's brothers in selling Joseph to the Ishmaelites—but so are the women: Sarah in tormenting Hagar and then convincing Abraham to send her away, Leah in her competitiveness with Rachel to have children, Miriam in objecting to Moses' marriage. Out of imperfect pieces we make something that is whole and even find a way to transmit the holy.

Something seemed to have been resolved, since Florence no longer raised the question of injustice and inequity. When she came in for her tenth appointment, a definitely more svelte Florence began the meeting with another one of her "pronouncements":

I've been trying to get really clear about who I am, both in the ways I come to God and the ways I live out my commitment in the world. I use language to think about who I am and to reach out to others.

Now Florence's view of language had taken on a whole new role. Language would be her principal tool for self-clarification, and yet language must always be experiential. No more "secondhand" God. She was determined to be a truth-teller, and the truth was to be found within her own life.

"There is something frightening about great joy," she said. "It is so expansive that our normal sense of self is shaken."

I didn't want to interrupt, but I strongly suspected that her "great joy" was related to her change in appearance. I noticed that her hair was no longer drawn back in a tight bun but had been styled to be attractively shaped around her head. Her new physical self was surely having some effect on her marriage, but I focused instead on her discussion of fear.

Fear is the most dangerous obstacle on the spiritual way. At *any* point, even far along, fear can make us turn back. We must not give in to it. Florence and I talked about the many different forms that fear can take. For example, we can feel increasing intimacy with God, feel the effortlessness of doing what we do, the way athletes attain "flow," and then realize that these so-called wonderful experiences have actually led us to be "too busy" to pray, to meditate, to make time to be with God. Florence's deep-seated honesty and determination to name things accurately had located the fear right inside the joy. When I called the fear "resistance," she immediately repeated the word, as if she were tasting it to see if it accurately portrayed her experience. She agreed and seemed heartened when she left.

I was surprised when, after opening up and broadening her understanding of what had brought her to spiritual guidance, Florence returned at our next meeting to the question of language. Was it part of the regression that I had warned against after her experience of joy? I withheld judgment and listened:

Language both determines what we call real and is determined by reality. We remember and focus on what we can name, but just what is nameable and what is not is not "given," that is, we get to choose what constitutes the real world. We can study what *is*, or we can make something and discover its *coming to be*. Our role in the creative process informs our understanding of the world around us.

I waited to hear what she was going to do with her own pronouncement. She reported on the coming together of the poet and the mystic. She told me about a poem she had written and how it had informed her about the process of creation in Genesis:

> Examining my own creative process gave the opening chapters of Genesis new meaning. I discovered that when I tried to write a poem. I allowed myself to use any poetic form—rhymed or free verse, sonnet or ballad or whatever. When I completed the poem to my satisfaction, then—and only then—did I ask myself, Did I begin with an idea? Where did the idea come from? After a while, did I have more than one idea in mind? What did I do with the other ideas? Did I discard any pieces of paper in the writing? (The overwhelming destruction of the Flood was never far from my consciousness.) Did I cross out any lines? words? erase? How did I decide I was finished? Did any part of what I wrote change form or change meaning after I had worked on it? Can I list the processes involved in writing the poem?
>
> Here is the poem in a rough-hewn version. Would it have been easier to write if I had thought I would never show it to anyone? I told myself I was writing a poem no one would ever see and judge, but it wasn't true, because all the critics and judges already live within me. To write, I need a willingness to look bad, incompetent, weak, out of control. So that's what I wrote about.

Why People over a Certain Age Don't Like Roller Coasters

Some say our center of gravity has changed.
We no longer like to be thrown around,
Scooped up, flung down,
scattered.
We know enough to be afraid.
But in our youth we found fear delicious.
All our anticipations had the shudder
of expectation.
Earthquake! Terror! But a sense of being
screechingly alive.
My stomach rises with the climb,
plummets down the steep hill;
can it take the curve?
Lack of control, but something is growing.
We start off trusting,
we learn to fear.
We are built for love,
we learn to hate.
We love being tossed in the air,
we learn to hold tight and not fly.
Can we just enjoy the ride?

When I began writing this poem, I had no idea what it was about. All I had was the title. I do not like roller coasters (and not just because I'm a person of a certain age; I have never liked them, ever since I once let myself be persuaded to try one). We can write about what we don't know. We create in order to understand what perplexes us, gnaws at us. Did I cross out any words? Yes: words, lines, whole couplets. How did I decide I was finished? I didn't; I'm finished only because I wanted to show it to you. I may still tinker with it. The meaning of what I was trying to say only gradually became clear to me.

I looked at my own creative process and recognized the components: terror, self-giving, love. I believed that I would read an account of creation very differently after I had tried to create something. I thought the only way to understand creation is from within my own creativity. I then read Genesis, chapters 1–5. My own feelings about what I had created (the poem) were echoed in the Scripture (it was good, or I saw from the start that it was flawed). The stages of Creation in Genesis are stages I myself can enter into: formless and void, and the spirit of God hovering over the water—the water being the depth of the unconscious. And "Let there be light" is the introduction of consciousness to this process.

Following this bravura performance, we both sat silently. I pointed out after a while that Florence's focus had been on the unification of the poet and the mystic, and on what her own creativity had shown her about the account in Genesis. But I was joyfully aware that far more had changed: she had entered into a magnificent adventure—regardless of what she chose to identify as the roller coaster—and had signed up for the ride.

8

RACHEL
A Teacher Explores Her
Spiritual Commitment

I had been seeing Rachel for over a year when she came for her appointment one dripping April day. She informed me that she was through "playing" at spirituality and now wanted to address it directly. I expressed my surprise. She had been seeing me every month, her prayer life had been going well—just what exactly had led to this statement? Rachel told me she had gone home for her twenty-fifth high school reunion.

Rachel had approached me the year before, when Bob, her young-adult son, was diagnosed with Hodgkin's lymphoma. Some people thought she was looking for a magic solution or was trying to relieve some guilt, but actually, the illness made her want to turn from the things she couldn't control, such as her son's serious disease, to what she could—her own spiritual growth. Although Bob's illness was currently under control, she knew that it could flare up again at any time. When I asked her about the high school reunion, she replied:

Unlike many of my classmates, I am still married to my first husband. At the reunion, each of us received an envelope containing a name tag, an enlargement of our high school yearbook portrait, an address book with the names, addresses, and e-mail

> addresses of all those who had registered, and a rather thick
> pamphlet titled "Returning after Twenty-Five Years," a collection
> of essays we had written twenty-five years earlier for Mrs.
> Gottesman, our old English teacher. Mrs. G., I soon learned—
> she's still alive and showed up briefly—had turned over these
> compositions, which she had had us write as practice college
> application essays, to a member of the reunion committee, who
> had done them up into a little booklet. Mercifully, Mrs. G.
> removed the names and any other identifying elements. She was
> always trying to get us to spell out our goals and objectives and
> to state our visions of ourselves. None of us expected to ever see
> those youthful daydreams again. And yet there they were,
> and in the context of our former classmates. A shattering
> experience!

Rachel paused and looked around the room, as if to reassure herself that she had not suddenly turned back into an adolescent. I asked
her how reading the essay made her feel.

> I was a little embarrassed by my youthful idealism and the opti-
> mism. But then I thought more and decided that reading my
> earlier vision was a wake-up call, telling me that I had unknow-
> ingly fallen into some kind of dullness, automatic pilot—I'm not
> quite finding the word. I just felt there was nothing in my life
> that I was serious about. When I was eighteen, I was completely
> alive—almost fearless.

"Really? Most eighteen-year-olds have some moments of bravado
and some periods of deep insecurity as they attempt to discover who
they really are."

> Well, yes, that too. But when I wrote that essay—. My former
> classmates read silently, and most kept their feelings to them-
> selves. Some, I'm sure, never even read the essays. A few ban-
> tered with each other about theirs. One fellow tore out his essay

and crumpled it up into a tight ball that he aimed at a waste-basket across the room. Everyone cheered and applauded when the paper ball entered the basket cleanly. I tried to tell myself that these were the essays that were written to get us admitted to our number-one college choices. No one dared to dream "small." We all had visions of producing great research and changing the world. I could not, at age eighteen, admit that twenty-five years later I would be a kindergarten teacher and live in the suburbs and be so—ordinary.

"But you like teaching kindergarten," I said.

"Well, yes, but it seems so unglamorous, compared to being a research scientist or a writer or any one of a number of challenging careers."

"Is that the thought behind your decision to take spirituality more seriously?"

Rachel twisted a strand of ash-blond hair around her finger. She had a habit of doing that, and even putting her hair in her mouth, when she was thinking of how to form what she was going to say. Her hair framed a pretty but somewhat careworn face that had no makeup or lipstick, but was adequately colored by her rich blue eyes. Finally, she said, "Well, I thought maybe this was God giving me a wake-up call."

"Were you asleep?" I asked somewhat disingenuously, but the question elicited a straight response:

"Not completely, but—now I'm more fully awake."

I asked her to explain.

I want to go off on a summer-long retreat, not like the Israelites fleeing the taskmasters in Egypt, fleeing the nightmare of Bob's illness or my self-doubts about teaching, but like the lover in the Song of Songs who says "draw me after, let us run." I want to enter into deeper and deeper intimacy with God.

"What about Bob's illness?"

"Bob is doing well and will be traveling in Europe this summer."

"And Herb?" (Herb was her husband, a salesman for an electronics firm.)

> Herb is fine—not happy about my desire for a summer-long retreat. We've spent summers together since Bob was little. Herb gets three weeks' vacation, and instead of taking them in one long block, he takes off Fridays and Mondays, so we have long weekends at the shore. He leaves for the city early Tuesday morning and is back Thursday for dinner. So this suggestion of mine really made him angry. He said I was turning him into a rival of God's.

"Is that true?"

> Herb has never been interested in my religious exploration and never encouraged it. There's no question about my commitment to Herb, but I feel I need time to process everything.

"Everything means what? Bob's illness? Your realization that you've been out of high school twenty-five years? Your curiosity as to where the next adventure lies?"

> The next adventure will, I hope, be my deepening intimacy with God, and it's the one that underlies all the others. I've been reading a lot, and I truly believe that I approach this task as seriously as any of the authors I've read.

She rattled off the names of some of the books she'd been reading: *Ascent of Mount Carmel*, by John of the Cross; *Showings*, by Julian of Norwich; *Autobiography*, by Teresa of Avila. I was uncomfortable that all her choices were from medieval Christian mystics, but we agreed to discuss them at our next meeting, in four weeks. Long after she left, I found myself thinking about this woman, whose intense desire for God may have made her more vulnerable to distraction than her more easygoing husband.

Rachel was a teacher who found tremendous support through her teaching during her son's illness. No matter how worried she was about him, she found she was single-minded when she came to class and could release her worries while she focused on the children she taught. Later, when he was on the road to recovery, she recognized what a gift her teaching had been. Still, when I saw her at the beginning of May, she was very troubled by a comment she heard one of the parents make to another as she brought the children down to be picked up: "I no sooner get here, leave him off, and get back home, when it's time to pick him up again. You'd think they'd keep them longer, or at least teach them something. My son tells me all they do is line up, sit down, line up again, take naps. If that's all they do, why do I need to send him to kindergarten?"

> I know the class works well. I know I'm teaching them how to love school, and most of the children are getting it. This is embarrassing, but I want to find out why the boy said this to his mother and defend myself. Why don't I just stop, really take in what is said and see if the criticism has merit or is just one mother having a bad day? It really shows me how much I crave my students' approval—maybe even everybody's approval. I have not learned to take criticism well.

Criticism at school, criticism from Herb—how did these attacks factor into her planning a long retreat that would absent her from her husband and daily life concerns? I reminded her of the bibliography she had rattled off the month before: John of the Cross (who was put in a dungeon by monks), Teresa of Avila (brought before the Inquisition but finally exonerated), Julian of Norwich, Meister Eckhart (brought before the Inquisition and saved from being declared a heretic only by his timely death). I handed her Martin Buber's *Ecstatic Confessions*. The book contains Buber's favorite mystical texts, including excerpts from each of the authors she had mentioned and many more. It was published fourteen years before his *I and Thou*, and perhaps, I suggested, this was an earlier stage of his spiritual development. It might even be considered juvenilia, although this is what he was reading and valuing at that point in his life. It is strange that our books can serve as markers of where we were in our own consciousness at the time we read them.

She immediately responded:

> Oh, I know exactly what you mean! I've come across books on my shelf that I used to love and now wonder why they were so important to me. I also see some of my underlining and wonder why I chose to highlight those sentences. Actually, one of the advantages of reading through the Torah every year is that you get to see how the book is always different because we're always different. But what has that got to do with Buber?

I asked Rachel if she had ever read *I and Thou*. She had started it, but she didn't think she had finished it. Anyway, that was many years ago.

I remarked, "There was a reason Buber went from the mysticism he highlights in *Ecstatic Confessions* to the dialogue of *I and Thou*. I know you're busy, but I would like you to try again to read *I and Thou*. Let's meet again in three weeks—that will still be May, OK? I think you should also know that when Buber's collected works were published, he would not allow his introduction to *Ecstatic Confessions* to be reprinted. It was the only work he refused to allow into the complete edition. He was clearly repudiating that work.

It was the last week of May when I next saw Rachel, and I was aware of the impending retreat. Nevertheless I started by talking about her teaching. That turned out very well because she remembered a story about getting quiet, a subject I was hoping to bring up with her:

> The first kindergarten class to which I was assigned had already had five teachers before I came. The students had come to believe that teachers came and left every few weeks and that it was their job to see that they really left. They had no great

reason to listen to the teacher. One day I gave each kindergart-
ner a piece of drawing paper. Once they finally got quiet, I gave
them each a crayon. As the quiet continued, they got two
crayons and finally a whole joyful array of color. They learned
they could earn richer experiences by getting quiet. What I
did—out of desperation in my first teaching job—I did, again
out of desperation, at this point in my life. I gave myself a day
that was like a blank piece of drawing paper. I gave myself hours
to grow quiet and slowly introduced the first color into my
world.

As Rachel and I talked she discovered that when she first recalled
the kindergarten story, she focused on getting down to essentials. She
didn't consciously reflect that the whole discipline problem had its
origins in their repeated experience of separation and loss. Initially
she was shocked to realize that that incident was emblematic of what
was happening in her own life—separation and loss. Her students
"recovered," and she got through the year. She could only hope that
she, too, would recover and move on. I now asked if she had read the
two Buber books. She had. What were the differences between the
two mysticisms?

> I'm not sure they are two mysticisms; it may be that they are
> two stages on the mystical path. I mean Plotinus and Eckhart
> and Teresa, they're all private and otherworldly, and late Buber
> is so involved in the world and with people and—
>
> Repeatedly, in reading spiritual books, I latch on to someone
> else's model of God's way in his or her life and try to apply it to
> my life. The premise is that we are unique, unrepeatable events.
> So why am I trying to be someone else? I must be myself.
>
> I really know that, but it is so hard to consistently live it. The
> spiritual life is so intangible, with so few road markers along the
> way. It is very tempting to see how other people do it, although
> we can never really understand their way. But trying to follow
> someone else's way always trips me up. Frequently it defeats me,

making me feel unworthy and inadequate, tempting me to give up altogether. So focusing on my own way becomes a necessity if I am not to get lost.

I reminded her that she is unique and so must take her way, guided by her relationship with God, and not get distracted by other people's ways. So what would it mean to be yourself?

The facts of our lives affect our spiritual paths. Most biographies of mystics list their books and their teachers but not their spouses and children. There cannot be a disembodied spirituality. How would my own spirituality read if I were not female, or had not been married, not had a son? Not spent years teaching kindergartners? I think I do learn a lot from my kindergartners. Remember that book a while back, *All I Ever Needed to Know I Learned in Kindergarten*? There really is something so basic in the lessons I teach the children. But it is so obvious I usually cannot see it.

"Like?"

Well, besides the examples in the book, noticing the first buds of spring. I've taken more walks with Kindergarten One in the past three weeks—and we're always holding a partner's hand. And celebrating the turning of the leaves in fall. And signing up for the privilege of feeding the goldfish or the gerbils. But it is all so ordinary.

"Wonderful and ordinary."
"Yes," she said, "but I'm not sure how to put the two together."
"Together we've seen that you really know, experientially, the reality of awakening, purgation, illumination, the dark night—but then there is a simplicity. I think, en route, you frequently felt special. But suddenly it is *ordinary*, and that's OK. It is almost as if the God you sought so focusedly is now almost not apparent because there is no

longer a difference between sacred and profane. When God is found everywhere—but not more in a particular building or a special text or a holy day—it is almost possible to confuse God's omnipresence with nonpresence. I'd call this normal mysticism, ordinary mysticism. But it has to be transmittable. People understand the special garb of the nun, the practices of chanting and meditating, special diets, silence and solitude—all these distinguish the spiritual way from everything else. How can you grasp that your ordinary way is the spiritual way?"

Rachel was very quiet. She began speaking almost to herself:

> At first I could not find my answer in and through other people. It was about myself and my relationship to God. Later, my relationship to God could be discovered, experienced, and expressed in and through my relationships to others—but I needed to go apart before I could discover God in and through everything.

"And now?"

> Herb may be right. Summer at the shore with times together and times apart, every tear I wipe on the first day of school— these are part of my way of coming to God.

Rachel was serious about leading a deliberate life—about making conscious choices that better shaped her for the spiritual way. She was attracted to mysticism—defined as "experiential knowledge of God." She didn't want the God she merely heard about, or accepted from authority or tradition, or even arrived at by pushing reason to its limits. She wanted to have an encounter with God. I applauded this quest and tried to encourage her. Rachel's progress on the spiritual way had been steady but then became complicated by her high school reunion. When I taught college undergraduates, I was highly aware of their problems in remembering who they were when the context in which they found themselves changed. Students going home for Thanksgiving suffered instant regression—they could not hold on to the still tender identity they had been shaping since arriving at school in September.

I had not anticipated that something analogous would happen to Rachel, but put back into the context of her high school days and seeing once again that passionate essay about saving the world had made her seek out some dramatic gesture that would demonstrate her spiritual commitment. Her focus on asceticism in the form of solitude, silence, and a long retreat came out of stories she had read and her rejection—not yet worked through—of aspects of herself. Most parents living through a major illness of a child must contend not only with fear for their child, but also their unconscious sense that maybe, in some unknown way, their partner is to blame. No matter how much science instructs us about the random distribution of certain illnesses, a less developed part of ourselves feels that bad things are not random but are punishments and judgments.

Rachel never voiced any of this, but I was aware that her interest in the retreat was not just a move toward God, but a move away from her husband. It was at this juncture that I found it especially necessary to guide her. There are profound dangers in the quest for an encounter with God. To make an analogy: There is a reason wine and other alcoholic beverages are called "spirits"—they transform our vision. A complimentary glass of wine in a restaurant enhances the meal, helps us digest, and doesn't cost anything. But there are other "spirits" that can change our whole perception of a meal, even make us forget our usual sources of nourishment, and could wind up costing us our entire vision of reality. So is the spiritual way like a complimentary glass of wine, or is it a drink far more potent? And what will it ultimately cost? With guidance, the cost will be everything by which we define ourselves, but the payoff will be huge.

So how do I proceed? Mysticism can be about the self (focusing on certain experiences), or it can be about loving God. The first is prideful and very dangerous. The second is what enables us to be ethical and loving. By directing Rachel to Buber and by reminding her of her experiences in teaching, I sought to emphasize that experiential knowledge of God is central, but it is not achieved through withdrawal from the world; rather, it is achieved through the natural route of love.

9

GLYNIS

An Adult Daughter's Reconciliation with Her Mother

For nearly two years, Glynis was playing a small supporting role in the Broadway production of a play, and all had gone well. At first she was grateful to have any part at all. Then she was able to get deeper and deeper into her character and to create new "business" to keep the part fresh. But after twenty-two months, she hit a block. She felt that she had developed her character as far as she could without actually changing the part. She knew the time had come when she would have to leave the play if she wanted to continue being engaged with her work.

We are not playing supporting roles—we are the stars in our own lives' stories. But we are not always sure to what extent we are improvising and to what extent we have become very convincing at repeating someone else's lines. And the day comes when we too feel we have hit a block. We do not see what we can do to refresh our roles, to revitalize our lives. Glynis complained to me of feeling a kind of deadness, that she was simply treading water to stay in place. She said that she loved her husband and her son, who was fifteen, and although they played major roles in her life, she was sure that her problem lay elsewhere. She decided that she was facing a spiritual question, but said she wasn't even sure what she meant by that.

Glynis's most distinguishing physical feature was her large and mobile mouth, whose corners turned skyward when she laughed and sank down into a Pagliacci face when she was sad. She had dozens of different eyeglasses, from which she chose one each day so that the frame complemented her outfit. Her lipstick color ranged from deep purple to none at all. I could never predict what hairdo she would wear on any given day: she might make her entrance in an elaborate, bejeweled updo or slip into my office in a simple ponytail held by an elastic. Her clothes similarly fell into a wide spectrum, though tending toward flowing scarves, overblouses, and peasant dresses or skirts. If I had to sum up in one word how she looked and dressed, it would be "dramatic," with a capital D. And as it so often happens, her outer appearance was just so much surface; hiding inside was a reserve and woundedness that became evident as soon as she started speaking.

She said that when she was feeling good, she was "very, very good." But the deadness she complained about could take over at any time, causing her to focus on multiple physical ailments that included recurring stomachaches and diarrhea, for which there seemed to be neither diagnosis nor cure, only holding operations; problems in balance, which resulted from mistreated childhood ear infections; and what she called "sick headaches"—not migraines, she assured me, because there were no auras or other common symptoms of migraine, but persistent, dull headaches that sometimes took days to recede.

The illnesses were real, but her suffering was exacerbated when she focused on them, anticipated them, and allowed herself to feel their full impact. At such times, her world was reduced to symptoms, fear, and simple self-maintenance. She had briefly mentioned all this to her doctor, who said it sounded as though she had had bouts of depression and asked if she wanted to see a psychotherapist. She did, for a few months, but felt she was getting nowhere and decided unilaterally to quit. I told her that I believed she could radically transform the effect of the symptoms if she could learn to shift her focus away from them and onto her life as part of a spiritual adventure to uncover her relationship with God. I also told her that going for spiritual guidance might be as hard for her as going for psycho-therapy, since both require a stripping away of defenses she has built up over many years. As a first step, I suggested she begin keeping a journal, if she felt comfortable doing that. At our second meeting a month later, she read to me from her notebook:

> "What aspect of myself do I disown? Weakness. I am weak, vul-nerable, afraid of rejection, afraid of losing control. I get so defensive when I don't feel well. I need to teach my lips to ask for help."

"But isn't that precisely what you are doing by coming here?" I asked.

She nodded, and went on:

> I know I need help, but even talking to my doctor took a Herculean effort, not to mention seeing the shrink. I never saw asking for help modeled in my family. My parents were self-reliant, so I felt guilty for not being as resourceful as they were and, I guess, for being a nuisance.

"Please elaborate," I said. "In what ways were you a nuisance?"

> The short answer is, just by needing help—parenting—just by being a child. But it became even clearer when I was sick. My mother would have to find a babysitter. Illness at my house was not a time to be nurtured, cared for, safely shepherded through the pain. Illness was a time of guilt, of shame, of a sense of my own intrusion into the more important world of my mother's appointments.

I asked Glynis whether she had been sick often in her childhood. She recalled that she was basically healthy, but that for one year she had one ear and throat infection after another, until finally her tonsils were removed.

"You must have had a very old-fashioned doctor, but at least it worked! What else do you remember about that year? Who cared for you when your mother wouldn't?"

She thought of the many babysitters, no single one of whom she could become attached to; of a neighbor she secretly wished she could move in with; of an aunt whom she normally saw only at family functions but who called her once or twice when she was home ill. And then she recalled her father's secretary:

> It was during that terrible year of repeated throat infections. My mother decided I was old enough to stay home alone—so I was alone in our apartment, recovering from strep throat and feeling weak and awful. But on every one of the eight weekdays of my illness, my father brought home a little gift that his secretary had sent along for me. One day it was a Louisa May Alcott book I had never read, another day it was a nosegay of assorted flowers from her garden, another, a sachet made of dried rose petals. On the fifth day, it was a miniature pie baked just for me now that I could swallow again, so I doubly appreciated it.

It was difficult but necessary to revisit her illnesses so that we could uncover why she so despised her own vulnerability. What she remembered about her childhood bouts with sickness made it clear that she associated them closely with how they hindered her mother's plans. Only after we had explored that issue could we begin the long journey of discovering Glynis's mother not simply in her role as "my mother" but as a person in her own right.

Since Glynis's own marriage, had there been any change in her response to illness? And how had she herself responded when her own son became sick? She ignored the first question and threw herself into answering the second:

> My overwhelming desire was that my son experience home as a place of safety. I wanted him to come trudging home from school on a cold winter afternoon and see the light in the

kitchen with a sense of both physical and emotional warmth. I wanted him to know that I'd be home and he would be cared for and safe.

We learn not only by having good role models, but by correcting inadequate ones. Glynis had managed, despite the demands of her career, to be there during the day when her son had colds, the flu, or just "didn't feel well." Except for Wednesday matinee days, she had made a point of being home every afternoon when he arrived from school—no latchkey kids for her! In the morning, she was always able to get him off to school before she returned to bed. If she had been her own child, I asked, how would she feel about her illnesses? She sat quietly for a long time before finally expressing her sympathy for the young Glynis. But she glossed over any anger she might have felt at her mother by saying that her mother merely was who she was—basically good, not perfect. I made a mental note to get back to Glynis's relationship with her mother.

Over the next few months we continued to talk about sickness, weakness, and vulnerability. Even though we explored the subject from many angles, I was surprised when Glynis told me:

I can now say that I have been *blessed* with a lifelong weak stomach. For years, I struggled to conquer what I felt was a serious flaw, not just in my body but also in my character. I gradually came to realize that my woundedness is a gift. I've learned to notice, to appreciate, and to give and receive gracefully. I've come to recognize that I am loved for being, not just for doing, and I've come to accept that areas of dependency and the capacity to suffer are also of value, that pain can be very helpful in effecting one's own transformation. It was a long journey from hating myself, disowning my body, and feeling guilty for burdening people with my illness, to recognizing my strengths as well as my vulnerabilities, to appreciating my body for withstanding the indignities to which it is subjected, and to seeing my illness as part of the entire human mosaic. We need to show ourselves the same compassion we show others; in fact, we cannot have real compassion for others unless we cut ourselves some slack.

I let her know how pleased I was with what she had said, although I was concerned that her understanding might be intellectual only and that she still faced a long journey before she could integrate this perspective into her whole life. But Glynis really was finding God in and through her relationship to her body. She spoke about sometimes coming to God in pain, and sometimes in gratitude, on days that were virtually painless. She began to see every day as an occasion to simply tell God how she felt and to then offer her fears or her gratitude to God.

If I had been designing a spiritual program, it would never have occurred to me to suggest that all guidees should be assigned weak stomachs, but I'm truly amazed at how this condition can lead to mindfulness. Now that I use it to help me become more aware, it doesn't feel the way it did before. I know this sounds daffy, but it feels as though God has been trying to get my attention for a long time.

Using her illness to guide her on her spiritual way finally allowed Glynis to talk about something other than sickness. Because she is an actor (she shuns the word "actress"), we explored where her art and spirituality interconnect. We agreed that fear and despondency pose dangers, not only on the spiritual way, but also on the creative path, because they hinder our ability to trust the world and be open to innovation. In describing her acting, Glynis spoke of feeling that she was in the dark, being pushed along, though to where she did not know. When she reflected on her last acting experience, she realized that the more she tried to impose control, the more she killed what was genuinely alive in the part. On her bad days, she felt that there was something untrue—she used the word "phony"—about her art and that what she was offering to the audience was valueless. She concluded that "the only way to act is to act creatively."

Many people attain spiritual growth using their religious traditions. For Glynis, however, spiritual growth meant artistic growth. In
using her creative talents, she had to call forth her emotions but control them with her reason. As one of her acting coaches said: "In order
to *act* drunk, you can't *be* drunk, because on stage you need the control that comes with sobriety." She quoted another of her teachers as
saying that acting requires love and discipline—the love that says "I
can't live without acting" and the discipline to work at it all day, every
day. She found it amusing that her spiritual growth seemed to have
the same requirements and concluded that a good method is a good
method, whether for acting or for growing spiritually.

The next time Glynis came to see me, she had the sniffles. "I'm not
sure if this is a cold or an allergy," she said.

> It used to come and go all the time. It almost seemed to me that
> when my stomach got tired of giving me grief, it told my nose to
> get stuffed up. I have a decongestant spray that works, but I use
> it only for performances, because I don't want to get addicted.
> Did you know that you can get addicted to nasal decongestants?

I asked Glynis if she really wanted to use this time to talk about
stuffed noses. She said no, but she wasn't sure where we had left off.

"Your mother," I said instinctively, although I then remembered
that we had been talking about acting. I realized that *I* was the one
who wanted to talk about her mother, and told her so. Of course, she
wanted to know what I was thinking, so I told her: "From your earlier
dismissal of your mother's lack of caring for you when you were sick,
and from other efforts to defend your mother, it's clear to me that
although you had set out on your own at eighteen, had been married
for almost twenty years, had raised a son into adolescence, had
attained enviable success in a difficult career, and had recently turned
forty, you have not yet moved away from home in one important
respect: you are still unable to tell your mother how angry at her you
were as a child. Instead, you've turned the anger on yourself and done
yourself damage. By saying that your mother 'was who she was—

basically good, not perfect,' shouldn't you at least be angry with God for bestowing this parent on you? Have you ever talked to God about it?"

She agreed that doing so might be a good idea, and we spent a raucous half hour during which she practiced telling God how angry she was. And although she confided to me that she had created a role for herself that would allow her to do that, she said that expressing the anger gave her great relief. It was, in fact, her first step toward becoming alive. Now she knew that she could be angry at God and still enjoy God's support. Could she also forgive her mother and mend their relationship?

Between jobs, Glynis taught drama and improvisation classes in after-school programs, both at the Y and at youth programs in various synagogues. She enjoyed the work, which paid very little, and she yearned for a steady acting job that would provide regular income and also give her a chance to explore many roles over a short period of time. ("Will there be anything else, Ms. Glynis?" she said, commenting on her own wish.)

Then one day, she came in with a broad grin and blurted out that she had been invited to audition for a New York repertory company that also did lots of improvisational theater. The group paid scale and was firmly based in an off-Broadway house, where it had been in residence for a dozen years. Someone in the troupe had seen her in the final months of her Broadway run, when she was desperately trying to keep the part new and fresh. The invitation was not an offer, but it was a delicious idea. But wasn't she doing more good in her after-school teaching, even though she didn't love the work the way she would doing improvisation?

We talked about the way gifted people sometimes feel guilty for exercising their gifts. What would Glynis advise one of the girls in her own drama classes who had received a similar invitation? She answered unhesitatingly that she would tell her to "go for it!" And then came the painful process of discovering why she had so much trouble giving herself the same advice. Did I think it had something to do with her mother?

How does an adult child transform her relationship to her mother —even disconnect from one that holds her back from her own growth? Judaism offers rich ceremonies of connecting parent to child, child to community, and bride to groom. There are, among others, the traditional Friday-night blessing of children by their parents, the rituals of circumcision and baby naming, and the rites for entering into the covenant of marriage. But what traditions help us disconnect? The bar and bat mitzvah services, which might be seen as fostering independence ("Now I am an adult"), are held at an age when children are far too young to go out on their own. These rituals actually serve to bind the youngster into the community ("Now I am eligible for counting in a minyan [i.e., a quorum for prayer]").

In many ways, of course, we are shaped by our ties to others, yet by no means do these ties define us. Each of us is unique, influenced and tempered by our own experiences, actions, thoughts, and decisions. In the Bible, a baby is usually named specifically to reflect some aspect of a parent's experience. For example, Isaac (in Hebrew, Yitzchak), which means "he will laugh," was given his name because his mother, Sarah, said that God brought her laughter in her old age. But in the Bible, a name is also thought to convey a person's essence, so Abram becomes Abraham when God establishes a covenant with him.

Although Jews believe that each person has a unique essence, there is no liturgy that reflects this tenet. People name us, in the sense of judging who we are, and that is indeed where our self-definition begins. But as we grow, our self-definition is determined more and more from within. Others necessarily "undername" us, that is, they simplify and trivialize who we are and what we stand for, because they cannot know all we have done, suffered, intended, or dreamt. We even undername ourselves, because we are more than all the roles we have taken on and played.

Glynis had internalized many of the inadequate names people had given her. "So where do I go on from here?" she asked.

I reminded her that she had managed to grow, and to love, and to form her own family, and that she was not repeating the errors she saw in her mother's behavior. Then, we tried to get a clearer picture of Glynis's mother. Glynis quickly warmed to her subject:

> Take my name: Most people are named after a beloved relative who died and whose memory you want to keep alive. Not me! I did not have a great aunt Gittel or anything like that. And Glynis isn't even a biblical name. I was named after an actress my mother admired. Explain that to a Hebrew school teacher! I was called Glyn, and most of my friends thought I was named after the good witch in *The Wizard of Oz*.

"So your mother loved acting. Is that where your own love for acting came from?"

> Now wait! Her acting is what I call performing, or playing in a masque, as a way of disguising her real feelings and thoughts. She always put a good face on things. When she was "on," which was whenever anyone outside the family was around, she was unreachable behind her mask. My acting is entirely different. When I act, I am vulnerable, as I reach deep within to find the truth of the character.
>
> My mother's audience is legion. This is a terrible thing to say, but—

Here she paused and looked desperately around the room, finally settling her gaze on the abstract purple-and-red painting on the wall to her left before continuing her thought.

> I often imagine that when she dies, a thousand people will have warm, funny things to say at her funeral, stories highlighting her charm and her humor. And I imagine that not one of those thousand will be a member of her immediate family. We never get to see the beloved side of my mother. The performance is for all of them, and no one, not even her family, has ever seen her human side.

"So there is a human side."

> There must be. After the company leaves and the door is closed, she is simply exhausted, like any actor after a good performance. Almost immediately, she quietly slips away to her room or to bed. In my childhood, it was the same thing: she was either playing a role or unavailable. I never was able to touch my genuine mother.

Glynis gritted her teeth and shook her head hard, as if to shake away the image of her mother becoming unavailable to her. Then she continued with another story of her mother's refusal to see her view of things:

> Many years ago, Bob—my husband—and I were going through a rough stretch. When I told my mother about it, she said I should get my hair styled, buy some new clothes, and stop offering my opinions all the time. I was furious and told her she was taking Bob's side. She said there were no sides to be taken. I told her that if Bob and I were to divorce, I was sure she would still send him birthday cards. She agreed and said, "I'd have to; he'd still be my grandchildren's father." I couldn't tell if she was enlightened or unfeeling.

"What did you want her to say?"

> I wanted to feel that she was firmly on my side. I've never felt that. When my son has a disagreement with his teacher, I cheerfully hate that teacher until the fight is resolved.
>
> Anyway, my mother's idea of acting was one big lie. In my own acting, by contrast, I am trying to get at some truth about the character. I draw on my own experiences, yes, but I put myself in the character's place and try to actually become her.

When Glynis came to see me next, she was wearing an antique watch on a gold chain around her neck. With all the quirkiness in her dress, she rarely wore jewelry, and when she did, it tended to be spare. This watch was beautiful and clearly expensive. I complimented her on it as she sat down in my office, and she told me that her mother had just given it to her:

> I can't believe it—my mother actually came to see me on an improv night at my theater, and after the performance, she visited me backstage. She made her usual excuses about its being late, she had to go home, but she wanted me to know that I had done well and she wanted me to have this watch. I love it. I first started asking myself what it meant that she gave it to me, but then I stopped and just told her that I loved it. Whenever I wear it now, I can recall that my mother—in her own way—was saying, "I love you."

10

LAURA

A Mother "Releasing" Her Grown Daughter

"It was scary to become a new mother, but there were so many books to guide you every step of the way—your baby's first year, the terrible twos. The books took you all the way through adolescence, and then they stopped! Where was Dr. Spock when you most needed him? How do you learn how to be a parent when your 'child' is an adult?"

That was Laura's question as she came to see me four years ago. I remarked that the Torah is very good at recounting the events surrounding the birth of a child, and it recounts the faithful coming together of adult children for their parent's burial. The hard part is in between—the part called Life. Laura had a gaunt look that immediately brought to mind the phrase "starving artist." She had a thin, pretty face and yellowish teeth. Her slacks and blouse were in good taste, if slightly shopworn. She smelled of cigarette smoke, and my windowless office gave me a bit of a trapped feeling, until the ventilation system sucked in most of the odor.

Laura was a divorced artist who earned her living doing social work in Brooklyn, where she lived in a small rental apartment. She told me that in addition to her job, she volunteered on Saturdays at a drop-in center for teenagers near her home. She shuddered as she saw her twenty-seven-year-old daughter, Marguerite, repeating some of the mistakes she herself had made. The way Laura described it:

> I'm so afraid my own bad marriage will poison her relationships with men. I kept telling her that her father was walking out on *me*, not her, but she was sure it was all her fault. She actually went to look for him after she got her driver's license. The shock was that he didn't want to see her, even though she assured him she was not looking for money. How can a father not want to see his own daughter? It was a terrible time, and I'm afraid it left scars. The men she dates don't appreciate her; she allows them to treat her thoughtlessly. I hate what my husband did to me and, even more, what he did to Marguerite—and what he may have done to her future.

Laura obviously loved her daughter and just as obviously feared her, because no one could hurt her as successfully as Marguerite could. I thought that spiritual guidance might allow Laura's love to grow, even while her agenda for her daughter diminished and finally just disappeared. It might also strengthen her interest in her own art and ease her involvement in her daughter's life. In the process, she began to recognize that there are different tasks for different times of life:

> Being a mother to an infant is easy: while it is physically demanding, at least you know what has to be done. My questions began once Marguerite went off to school. How much should I help her? How much should I demand of her? School was confusing, and there came a time when she was studying things I didn't know, so I couldn't help her even if I wanted to. I was an art major in college, and I didn't take my other courses too seriously. I thought I'd learned about social relationships, but today's world is so different from the one I knew as a child that I can't figure it out at all. Is everything I know out of date? If so, why go on?

Laura sounded despondent, but her half-smile at the end of her question suggested to me that she really did want to go on; she just needed some help in finding the inner strength. So I challenged her view of herself: "But look at the young people you meet at the drop-in center. I'll bet they think you have interesting ideas. You do unto them what you pray someone is doing unto your daughter. Sometimes we can't mother our own children; we can only hope that someone else is doing what needs to be done."

Laura thought of various surrogate mothers she had found "en route to growing up." Then she caught herself:

> Wait, why "en route to growing up"? I'm supposed to be an adult, but I'm still looking for older women as role models and guides. I have to smile when I think of the "tea ladies," three elderly women who live together in an old Victorian at the end of my block. Occasionally I shovel out their driveway in winter, and they invite me in for tea and truth. And there are some of the older women at work. Actually, the only arena where I *don't* look to my elders is in my painting. I like the energy and daring of the young artists.

Laura's close connection to her daughter was certainly an arena in which her relationship to God could be examined and highlighted. Marguerite lived in California and had bounced from graduate school (without finishing a degree) to a series of jobs, and with every change came a new apartment and a new boyfriend. My objective was to have Laura continue to scrutinize her relationship to Marguerite, but to look through it to her enduring relationship with God.

Over time, Laura could see that we probably never stop wondering "Do you love me?"—first about our parents and then about our children. But the connection between people of two generations should be one in which each enables the other to be independent—a relationship of release. As Laura spoke of her relationships, the story of the *Akeidah* kept coming to mind. One of the most troubling narratives about the parent-child relationship in the Torah, it describes the binding and near-sacrifice of Isaac by his father:

> Some time afterward, God put Abraham to the test. He said to him, "Abraham," and he answered, "Here I am." And He said, "Take your son, your favored one, Isaac, whom you love, and go to the land of Moriah, and offer him there as a burnt offering on one of the heights which I will point out to you." (Genesis 22:1–2)

I knew I would have to discover why that story kept pressing itself onto my consciousness as I worked with Laura. I decided to trust my intuition by asking her to think about this passage and come back to me next time with all her reactions to this story. Laura was delighted with the assignment. She liked being the bright student again. Meanwhile, I set myself the task of trying to understand why I was asking Laura to examine this text.

I knew that the *Akeidah* was not a passage Laura would have chosen voluntarily. Who was Laura in this story? Did she identify with Isaac, with Abraham, or perhaps with God? But which God: the one commanding Abraham to sacrifice his son, or the one telling him not to harm the youth? Although I was not sure why, I felt strongly that the *Akeidah* was a story she needed to confront. I decided to simply wait and see what would happen.

When I next saw Laura, she seemed eager to begin talking. She settled in and started in on the assignment to think about the *Akeidah*. She began in a way that was consistent with her years of painting, that is, she set the scene physically; then she entered into the character of Abraham:

> Abraham carefully walked up the sun-drenched hill that led to Mount Moriah—which would later be the mountain on which the Temple is built. He saw his son's anxiety, heard the long silence, and noted the effort with which Isaac asked, "Where is the sheep for the burnt offering?" What did it cost Isaac to ask that question? Abraham felt the tension in his own gut and Isaac's trembling—and then he raised his knife.

I waited, wanting to hear what she would do with this scene, but she laughed uneasily. "Then I get stuck," she said. "What exactly did you want me to think about when you gave me this text to read?"

I was unconvinced by her "stuckness"—she probably didn't like what she was thinking and therefore could not say it aloud. I was also aware that she wanted to blame me for her own discomfort. I could back off and simply change the subject, decide that assigning that text had not been effective, but something suggested to me that it had worked very well. Laura respected intuition, so she tried to reflect further on the text. She finally looked at me frankly and asked for help—could I ask some leading questions or suggest ways of entering into the text? I mentioned the next point very cautiously, keeping in mind that Laura's daughter was twenty-seven: "The Rabbis tried to clean up the story, so they decided that Isaac was twenty-seven years old. That way they did not have to deal with him as a trusting child, and they could make him complicit in the event. Would making him an adult change the way you feel about the story?"

Laura was quick to answer:

> But that's outrageous! Whether the kid is six years old or twenty-six or whatever, Abraham has the firestone and the knife—what sort of chance does Isaac have? This blame-the-victim thing—it infuriates me!

I agreed, saying that I also found it less than useful that the Rabbis whitewashed the full horror of the story. But I was also aware that an important insight could be seen in the Rabbis' approach. Laura, and other parents of adults, try to convince themselves that their offspring are facing a harsh and dangerous world, when it is really the parents who are facing something terrifying: the inevitable loss of their children. Frequently, the Torah teaches lessons in reverse: Lot's daughters supposedly seduce their inebriated father so that a new crop of children could take the place of those destroyed in Sodom and Gomorrah. But reading this story today, we know that it is almost always the drunken fathers who sexually attack their daughters and then try to blame their victims for seducing them. I paused and then asked Laura if she could read the *Akeidah* as if it, too, were reversed. She wasn't sure what I meant, so I explained: "If the story of the *Akeidah* were reversed, then Isaac, the whole object of Abraham's longing ('O Lord God, what can You give me, seeing that I shall die childless' [Genesis 15:2]), would be the one doing the sacrificing. He is sacrificing his relationship to his father, by leaving him in order to become his independent self. Indeed, Isaac is never again mentioned in the Bible in conjunction with Abraham except at his father's burial."

I asked Laura, "Is it Marguerite's independence that you fear? And where is your relationship with God in and through all your dealings with your daughter?"

Laura thanked me for the chance to look at this text in a new way but steered the conversation to something less troubling during the remaining minutes of the session.

Several meetings later, Laura announced that her daughter was seeing a new man and probably living with him. I asked how she knew and, more important, why she knew. Marguerite's relationships with men are hers and hers alone, and Laura should stop approving or disapproving. "Just release her," I said, more forcefully that I'd meant to. I suggested to Laura that she keeps getting hauled back in. She tried to excuse her behavior by alluding to the fears raised by her own failed marriage and the great pain it must have caused her daughter.

Because she raised the concept "pain," we started discussing what it had led to in her own life and what she hoped it could lead to in her daughter's. Laura's marriage had been filled with psychological and, finally, physical abuse, and it had taken great courage for her to break away. During years of economic hardship, she had to put her artistic pursuits on hold in order to earn a credential that would qualify her for a regular salary and health benefits. With no help from her ex-husband (in fact, no contact at all), she had seen Marguerite through college and through her subsequent move out West. She hated the physical distance between them and felt uncomfortable using e-mail.

I asked Laura how old she was when her daughter was born. She admitted that she was younger than her daughter is now but protested that this generation is so young and immature. And what had led to her own growing and maturing? "The pain I had to deal with early on," she said.

I waited a moment, then asked, "Did you hear what you just said? 'The pain *I* had to deal with.' Don't stand in the way of your daughter's dealing with her pain."

I pointed out to Laura that she will be the last to see and recognize her daughter's growth, but chances are that Laura's brother and sister have already seen it, as well as a few cousins. She seemed a little bewildered. Suddenly she had acquired more space emotionally, and she wasn't sure what to do with it. "My job is to focus on me, isn't it?" she said.

> Look, I'm really trying to find God in all of this, and I haven't forgotten what you—I mean—what I said about the *Akeidah*, but this man is coming on too strong. He reminds me of my ex. I just have a bad feeling about him, and Marguerite is three thousand miles away.

Laura phoned me urgently a few weeks later, after her daughter had stopped seeing the new boyfriend, saying that she really needed to talk to me. When I saw her the next day, I pointed out that Marguerite had not stayed in a bad situation, and wasn't it good that she had worked things out without help from Mom? But she told me that Marguerite was terribly unhappy, now that she was without a man, and Laura wondered what she should do.

"OK," I said, "you thought you'd cut the line and that Marguerite was happily—or unhappily—swimming along, when with one phone call, you're the fish once again and Marguerite has skillfully reeled you right back in. You were 'hooked' by your daughter's plaintive tone and by the fantasy that you could make everything right."

Laura's concern for her daughter was genuine, but it was also concern for her own status, both in their relationship and in the world. As she explained it:

I guess I'm not sure who I am when I'm not Marguerite's mother. I've spent so much of my life raising her and caring for her and trying to make ends meet and—it's hard to change focus.

It was good to get away from Marguerite and return to Laura's thoughts about herself. I realized we were not done with the *Akeidah*; she had come away with an insight, and it was surely a visceral one. But there was more for her to explore. Although both her parents were dead, Laura was a daughter; she was also an ex-wife, a mother, and an artist. In each of these roles, I said, she faced questions about the relationships of creator to creation and creature to creator.

"Those are exactly the kinds of questions I love to tackle," she said. "I guess it's the artist in me." She gave the last phrase some extra emphasis by saying it a touch more slowly than the first. The same little smile at the end, which I'd seen before, was this time meant to reassure me that she knew it took a certain hubris to call herself an artist. But it also told me that "artist" is an important identity for her, regardless of what she said about her primary role as Marguerite's mother.

Because of Laura's unwitting self-identification, I decided to use the idea of artistic creation to approach her separation from her daughter. I discussed with her the different modes of creation, applying them, once again, to the story of the *Akeidah*.

Each of our creations involves a relationship. In procreation, it is that of parent to child, a connection that can be fraught with problems but that also includes deep resonances of love. The second form of creation is manufacture, or artistic creation. I explained that manufacture referred to any form of creation that used preexistent materials, as her own painting did. The relationship of artist to creation is one of care and deliberation, but also one of judgment. Laura nodded in agreement and spoke of the many canvases she simply turned toward the wall, deciding to face them again some other day, or maybe never. She spoke of these as her "abandoned babies" and then stopped, shocked that it might have something to do with her relationship to Marguerite.

I pointed out that a canvas cannot complete itself, but a daughter can. Your paintings cannot get any further, much less become completed, without you, but Marguerite can find surrogate mothers, as you did, or boyfriends, or experiences at work, or she can take a class. A great many paints touch her surface and even enter into the deep structure of who she is.

Suddenly, Laura looked at me accusingly: "We weren't going to talk about Marguerite. We were going to talk about the *Akeidah*."

"Fine," I agreed. "Do manufacture and the sorts of things that can complete themselves come into play in the relationship between Abraham and Isaac?"

> Well, judging from Abraham's actions, he thinks Isaac is his work of art. He believes that everything Isaac thinks or does or says has its origin in Abraham and can be controlled by him.

"I agree," I said. "Even Ishmael, the brother who might have played with him and given him a different perspective, is sent into exile. Abraham believes that only he can shape the lad. He doesn't even consider the possibility that Isaac could have his own essential nature or that he could have his own relationship with God."

Laura rummaged in her pocketbook, pulled out a cigarette, and looked around the room. Seeing no ashtray, she pushed the cigarette back into the pack, breaking it in the process. "I'm not Abraham. I'm not!" she said.

Again I agreed with her, and we finished the hour talking about some of the canvases turned toward the wall.

When Laura was late for our next meeting, I became concerned, afraid that our previous session had been too challenging. I waited in my office praying to be guided, when she knocked on the door.

"Subway tie-up," she volunteered.

I looked her over carefully, and she seemed fit. I waited, silently praying, to see what she would say, and when she spoke, it was to ask, "Are we done with forms of creation? Are we done with the *Akeidah*?"

I asked her if she felt finished. She simply said, "If there's more to be said about it, let's do it."

I explained that the third form of creation applies only to God. It is called *creatio ex nihilo*, creation out of nothing, so it is less a form of creation than a negation of the two previous models: procreation and manufacture.

"So does that mean God is neither a parent nor an artist?"

Instead of answering her question, I asked another: "What would it mean to have a creator who takes no parental or artistic interest?" Before I could mentally add the question mark at the end of that sentence, she retorted:

> Hey, wait a minute! I have sat through a hundred repetitions of prayers on Yom Kippur, and that's not what the prayer book says. It reads, "God is our Father, our King," and we are to God— that is, *God the artist*—"as clay in the hand of the potter who shapes it or breaks it at will." Why do we even need creation "out of nothing"?

I replied, "It comes from the account of Creation in Genesis, chapter 1, 'And God said . . . ,' which is taken to mean that God created by word alone. But Genesis, chapter 2 gives an entirely different account: God formed humans from the dust of the earth (which is why they say from dust you came and to dust you shall return) and then breathed into Adam the breath of life. In this version of the story, you have both those forms of creation at once: God is an artist (and your reference to potter is apt here), and God is a parent—of sorts—by breathing into us the breath of life, that is, some of God's unique essence."

Again without a moment's hesitation, Laura said that she liked this model of creation much better than *ex nihilo*: "I don't like creation out of nothing."

"Whether you like it or not, is there any reason to think further about it?" Like the proverbial terrier, I wouldn't let go of my challenge: "Can you think of anything we can learn about our own roles as parents and artists from creation that is neither parental nor artistic?"

Laura chewed that over for a bit, but finally said no, she didn't see what I was driving at. And although I hate giving speeches when I'm doing spiritual guidance, I pressed on, as much to bounce my own thoughts off Laura as to help her. "I believe that *ex nihilo* is also an ingredient in both procreation and manufacture," I said. "To go back to the *Akeidah* (as you say, my favorite story), Abraham's call to sacrifice Isaac forces him to transcend both procreation and manufacture by entering into this third way. You agree, I'm sure, that as a parent, Abraham was far too controlling. But we don't pass on our faith by rigidly enforcing it. What we try to pass on is our faith *in* faith, allowing it to take on different forms and shapes in the new life that nurtures it."

"Wait," she said, "I want to take notes."

I waited as Laura fished a small notebook out of her pocketbook. Now I was really beginning to regret that I was using her as a sounding board for my own ideas, but at least I was getting clear why the *Akeidah* story held such fascination for me. But Laura was giggling with glee, either because she could enjoy being a student again or because she was really getting into the story. I picked up where I'd left off: "When Abraham is told that his seed will be 'as numerous as the stars in the sky,' he takes the promise literally. He places all his hope in his two sons, Ishmael and Isaac. But with his expulsion of Ishmael and the order to sacrifice Isaac, we assume that his offspring will not be biological. Manufacture is not, of course, an option. So how can we reproduce ourselves nonbiologically?"

Laura brought me back to earth:

> You know, I often feel as if I know absolutely nothing when it comes to giving Marguerite advice, but I'm very capable of advising and helping the kids in the drop-in center. I'm not parenting them biologically *or* molding them out of clay, but I am parenting them. Look, I'm beginning to get it. Let me start our next meeting with all I can put together from our discussion of creation and the *Akeidah*.

Laura was smiling when she came in the following week. She was clearly eager to test out her ideas:

> Parenting is one of the areas in which we learn to get out of the way and identify with something beyond our own life and efforts. In that sense, procreation takes a backseat to our ability to focus on something other (and sometimes, it is *really* other!).
>
> In my artwork, I've learned how much effort and care it takes to create something, and then how transient the result usually is. Very little, if anything, that I've created will outlast me— heck, in most cases it doesn't even outlast my own judgment as to its "high" quality. I've come to realize that products are not central to the creative process and that to find meaning I must enter into creativity for its own sake. Through this process, I've reinforced my belief in the description of chaos offered in Genesis: "The earth was unformed and void, and darkness was upon the face of the deep; and the spirit of God hovered over the face of the waters." I really know that's true—I've experienced the formlessness, the void, and the darkness many times, and I've also experienced a guiding presence.

She knew what procreation is and what manufacture is, so I used these two forms of creation to help explain the third form. Now, I hasten to admit that I don't know, nor does anyone else, exactly what *ex nihilo* creation consists of, but I used the other two forms of creation to present a model of how it might work. We can think of manufacture as controlling, and giving birth as releasing. Perhaps we can think of *ex nihilo* as a combination of the two, that is, alternating control and release. I drew the analogy with breathing: we breathe in (control) and breathe out (release). According to Jewish mystical tradition, the four-letter name of God in Hebrew, spelled *yod, hei, vav, hei*, signifies that God, like our very breath, is omnipresent: *yod* (inhale), *hei* (exhale), *vav* (inhale), *hei* (exhale). We experience God as both immanent (when we draw God into ourselves) and transcendent (on releasing the breath of life and the self).

This reflection on breathing hints at a major question in our love of God. The breath we exhale feels intimate—we had it within us, circulating throughout our bodies—and yet, just a moment before, it was outside, waiting for us to inhale. What is the source of the love with which we love God? Is it our own deepest nature, or is it outside waiting for us to take it in?

When I next saw Laura, three weeks later, she wouldn't let me open my mouth. She held up her hand to silence me and then put down her pocketbook and placed her jacket over the back of the chair. When she was finally settled in her seat she looked at me, grinned, and said:

> The *Akeidah*—are you ready for this?—is a lesson in exhaling, in letting go. You only have what you are able to release. The first step in resuscitating someone who has stopped breathing is to push the air out of the lungs so that oxygenated air can flow in. In *Baby and Child Care*, Benjamin Spock describes breath-holding spells in infants and toddlers—Marguerite had them. The instant the child passes out from holding its breath, it automatically starts to breathe again. In fact, the recommended treatment is to let go—let the episode run its course, and the child will soon tire of the whole thing and stop having breath-holding spells altogether.
>
> There is a direct connection between the physical and spiritual processes of letting go. When we feel depressed, what we most want to do is curl up into a ball (our singular way of circling the wagons), yet at this moment of vulnerability, that opening up would be the most helpful thing to do. In other words, exhale and you shall be filled. Creativity is about exhaling, letting go, opening up.

Laura stopped and we both just sat there, grinning. Then she continued:

> Another surprise: you won't believe what I've been doing this week. No, I did not phone Marguerite or buy a plane ticket. I

turned all my abandoned canvases away from the wall and spent a while just studying them. And then I began painting, like mad, with a passion I haven't felt in—well, I don't know how long. I don't quite understand what's happened, but I do know I feel alive.

I knew with certainty that Laura would not always feel this alive and that doubts would arise. In the following meetings, we took the discussion even further, looking especially at a specific form of creation *ex nihilo* that is described in Lurianic Kabbalah, a work of Jewish mysticism. If we start with the belief that God is All in All, or infinite (that outside of which there is nothing), there could be no independent world. But under this form of creation, called *tzimtzum* (contraction), God voluntarily contracts, thereby creating space for the universe. In other words, we could say that God abandoned a region within God's own self, but then returns to the region through creation and revelation. I pushed Laura, who had become very courageous in thinking about hard questions, to examine what voluntary self-limitation meant to her in her creative roles as mother and artist.

> There is a lot of pain in love. Actually, that statement could be expanded to a whole book. Love, the greatest joy, is also the source of the greatest pain. As painful as it has been, though, I'll take the way of the tempering through parenthood. I know what caring costs, and I also know how it imbues everything with meaning and value. I choose to love.

Laura reached into her voluminous pocketbook and pulled out a short prayer that she had written:

> Thank you, God, for giving me parents whose imperfect love was still good enough to keep me from being mortally wounded; and for bestowing on me all the love that has nourished me on my way; and, above all, for nurturing my awareness of your love,

which makes all my grasping after other things unnecessary. I am loved, I have been loved, it is in love that I have my being.

Not surprisingly, Laura soon fell into despair once again. We spend a lot of time building structures of support when we are feeling good so that they will be in place when next we need them. Marguerite had quit her job, and Laura was torn between wanting to tell her to move home, sending her money for her rent, or just waiting: "If I cannot help those closest to me, what *can* I do?"

The answer is that we cannot help others. We can be there for them, we can pray for them, and we can wait and trust. But Marguerite must work through her life alone—as must Laura, as must everyone else. During all those years of marriage, she was able to do nothing about her ex-husband's unending depression and subsequent rages. She had had to fight fiercely to hold on to her own positive feelings. She had not been able to make her daughter have a deeper sense of self-worth. We can do nothing but love and wait and trust and pray.

Laura then read to me from her diary, which was written on some blank pages in her sketchbook:

> Let go: as mother, as artist, as daughter. When all of this is gone, who or what remains? Did I really write this a year ago? I am not my roles; in fact none of my roles as I originally understood them remains.
>
> I thought perhaps I would lose my job—but then I would still paint, for the birds and the trees. But instead, my daughter has attacked me with a suffering I thought I couldn't bear with dignity. She berated me for not supporting her when she quit her job. And then I became more aware of the struggle between generations and could almost relish the attacks. And I began to attack those badly neglected canvases.

Now, a year later, she can affirm that not only does something remain—life and more life and a reason to get up in the morning—

but it is deeper and more potent than ever before. This excitement is what she is slowly coming to discover and claim. Parenting is one of the strongest contexts for learning how to let go and trust. It is where we must learn to release our children, whom we deeply love, and forego any agenda we have for them. Laura feels more and more strongly that she must not interfere in Marguerite's life, that her daughter will grow as she must, and that all will truly be well. At the same time, she has slowly developed techniques to avoid being drawn back into her daughter's further drama. And in releasing her daughter, Laura can now see a larger world where her creative caring can be expressed.

II

MARTIN

A Priest Discusses a Personal Problem

I was surprised when I heard from Father Martin. I had gone to him for spiritual direction, as he called it, more than twenty years ago, when I first sensed that I was being called to something but didn't know what it was. I told Father Martin that I was Jewish, but that no spiritual guides of my faith existed at the time and the rabbis whom I approached could not help me.

Martin—he insisted I call him that—was a Roman Catholic chaplain at a college outside Boston. He had written several books that I had found useful. We worked together for two years, after which he was going abroad for an extended stay, so he recommended me to a colleague of his. Except for an annual exchange of notes written on greeting cards, Martin and I had not been in touch for some twenty years. I scheduled an appointment for him, although I could not imagine why he wanted to see me. Was he retiring and moving back to his order's religious foundation in the Midwest? Had he been curious as to whether I was following his way of doing spiritual guidance? (I had, at the start, but spiritual guidance has a way of taking on a life of its own, and now my approach incorporates what I have learned while working with five spiritual guides, together with a large dose of homegrown technique.)

Father Martin, now in his late fifties, looked as trim and athletic as I'd remembered him. His brown beard now bore touches of gray, and his brown hair, combed straight back, had turned silver. We hugged, and after a few pleasantries, he asked me about my life with God. I could answer succinctly and honestly that it had been going very well. Remembering that he drank herbal tea, I offered him a cup, which he politely waved off, even after I mock-assured him that it was kosher. He told me he needed to speak with a non-Catholic, and I seemed to him a logical choice, indeed, "the only logical choice," because he knew he could trust me to both listen sympathetically and advise him honestly. I suddenly got very nervous, wondering what awful problem was coming, and I actually clutched the edge of my desk to keep my balance. But when I turned to him my face was composed, and I uttered the words I had said so many times: "Anything said in this room, whether by you or by me, stays in this room." And so we began.

Martin had loved college, he said. His GPA was close to 4.0 (here I sensed in him a tinge of embarrassment for boasting), and he had played varsity basketball—even now, I could imagine him in that role. His family expected him to become a priest, but he was enjoying his late teen years so much, he was hoping the idea would just float away. He hesitated, so I encouraged him to continue:

> I knew I was supposed to be a priest, called to be a priest, but it was the last thing I wanted to think about. College was a time when the whole world opened up for me. I was quite popular; the girls thought I was good looking. I traveled to many different campuses with the team, and the thought of leaving all that behind for seminary was not appealing. In my senior year I had a serious girlfriend, Kathleen, and after one of the times we were together she got pregnant. The day she told me—I don't know— every sort of thought went through my head: now I'll never have to be a priest; now I'll go to hell; I don't want to marry. I don't know how long I was silent, but she told me categorically that she had discussed it with her parents, that she was going to

have the child, and that she didn't want to see me anymore—in fact, ever again. I knew in my heart of hearts that I didn't want to marry her, but I hadn't anticipated this rejection. Later, of course, I realized that she had sensed my feelings and had pushed me aside before I could dismiss her. I never did see Kathleen again, or even hear about her, but the summer after graduation I finally decided to enter seminary, probably out of guilt for getting her pregnant and then running away from my responsibilities. In the course of my priesthood, I've been in psychotherapy, and I've been a spiritual guide for many of the priests in their first years of formation. I had managed to push Kathleen and her pregnancy into the far recesses of my memory.

"And then?" I had a pretty good idea of what was coming, having long ago read Erich Segal's *Man, Woman and Child*, in which a man's love child suddenly turns up.

I got a letter saying that Kathleen had died of breast cancer and had, on her deathbed, told her daughter that I was her biological father. The daughter is now married, has a child of her own, and would like to meet me. I'm terrified. I abandoned Kathleen for God—no, that's not fair, I'd never let my novices get away with such self-serving excuses. I really wasn't ready to get married, so after trying half-heartedly to follow up on Kathleen after college, I simply put the whole relationship behind me. When the Internet came into being and we got online at the house, I went to one of those high-school-yearbook sites hoping I could locate her and at least find out whether she had had a son or a daughter. I'm a hopeless case when it comes to technology, or—again—maybe I didn't want to find out, but I never did locate her.

"How much of this do the people in your order know?"

I told the novice master when I was in formation. Since then, no one in the order knows, although my novice master probably talked at the time with the bishop. I've had spiritual directors all these years, but I never even thought to discuss Kathleen with any of them. It was almost as if the whole thing had never happened.

"Why aren't you discussing it with your current spiritual director?" I asked. He shifted in his chair, then replied:

Well, you can imagine that I feel terrible about it, and I certainly will bring it up in confession, as I did at the time. But my confessor will say the same thing my spiritual director will say: "Pray, and the answer will come to you."

That was pretty much what I intended to say, too. Instead, I parried: "And what makes you think I'd say something different?"

I hoped that as a woman and a Jew, you could bring a different theology to bear on the issue. I probably will talk to my spiritual director at some point, but right now I need immediate advice. Should I agree to see her? Can I even refuse? How can I face her?

I know I'm not totally evil. This one act doesn't negate all the good I've done for the past twenty-five years as a priest, but I've built on a pretty rotten foundation. I'd love to get all cognitive with you and talk about free will and destiny and that wonderful line in Saint Augustine, "Lord, make me pure, but not yet." That could have been my motto in college. My life eerily resembles Augustine's, but my theology is anything but Augustinian. I feel so stuck. I haven't even answered her letter. I almost wish I could return it marked "Return to Sender: Addressee Unknown."

"Isn't it possible that this is a profound gift for you? God's giving you a chance to get it right? *Have* you prayed about it?"

"Ouch! No," he said, "I haven't. Why do twenty-five years of training fly out the window when it's time to apply it to your own life?"

How right he was! I answered, "Because we are created to need and support one another. I frequently tell my guidees just what I need to tell myself, but I can't do it for myself."

"You really have learned well from me," he said, lightening the atmosphere in the room.

I then asked him to tell me where God was in this story and how he might turn to God as he tried to discern how to respond.

> I believe that God wants me to think about the differences between men and women and to learn from my predicament. Here I was trying to grow spiritually, and all the while she had this life growing in her. I, as a man, could turn the whole affair (oops, no pun intended) into an intellectual problem, but she had no choice: for her it was a real-world, physical issue (oops, again!)

I asked him to tell me more about her. Did she marry? Did or does her husband know? Was the child raised Catholic? He pulled from his pocket a limp piece of paper, whose creases tore slightly when he unfolded it. It was the letter, and it had obviously been read and reread many times in the past two days. It was only one page long, written on one side in neat, slanted handwriting. He recited it, almost from memory:

> "My name is Sandra Rollins. Two weeks ago, my mother—Kathleen Magill Rollins—told me on her deathbed that she didn't want any secrets between us. She told me then that the man she had been married to, who had raised me, and who died of heart failure three years ago was my father in every sense but one, and that you were my biological father. My feelings at that time were already all tied up in knots because she was dying. Her revelation came as a complete surprise and threw me into complete turmoil, from which I haven't yet recovered. When I asked her why she hadn't married you, she said because she had married my father. I don't know if you would be interested in

meeting your daughter or your granddaughter, but if you are—"
here she gives me her address, phone number, and e-mail
address. I can't begin to think how to answer that letter. I've
racked my brain trying to remember if I knew anyone with the
last name Rollins, but no one comes to mind. I know that isn't
the point, but I can't seem to focus on the real issue.

"I imagine you discussed all this back during your noviceship," I
said.
He nodded.
"So it's not a question of confession, or plan, or anything like that."
He nodded again, and continued:

But I had no idea what I was confessing to back then. I had gotten a woman pregnant, but I didn't draw out the conclusions: that
there would be another life that had to be cared for and nourished and brought into adulthood. I never, in all those years, imag-
inatively tried to enter into Kathleen's world. Was she alone when
my daughter was born? Was she frightened? I managed to think
nothing, feel nothing, and no one ever called me on it. I guess, in
part, that's why I had to talk to you. How much of my—and my
priests'—insensitivity came from our being male, and how much
from being priests? I think I learned more from this one letter
than from all those years of spiritual direction. That line, about
Mr. Rollins's being her father in every sense but one, really got to
me—and I have the nerve to call myself Father Martin.

"You must answer her today," I said. "She should not have to wait,
wondering whether or not she'll ever hear from you."
"OK," he agreed, "I'll write to her."
"Fine, but do it by e-mail, so she'll get her answer right away."
He asked me if he could send a draft of his e-mail to me first so I
could edit it.
"No," I said, "this is between you and her. We can talk more and get
clear on what you want to say, but then it is between the two of you."

"I feel so guilty."

"Your guilt is a luxury. Here is a woman whose mother died just two weeks ago, and her father died three years ago. She's an orphan, but you're still focused on yourself, not on what she might need and what you could give her."

I thought immediately that my anger at his unfeeling reaction had gotten the better of me and that I'd spoken too harshly. But he took what I said to heart:

> I never thought about it that way, that guilt can be a luxury. Sometimes I'm clear about that when I'm working with novices: they're so good at self-flagellation, I have to remind them there's work to be done. That's it, isn't it? I need to discover what work there is to be done and this time stay focused. Thank you, you really have been helpful. I'll get back to you.

That evening I received an e-mail from Martin: "This is a copy of the e-mail I sent to Sandra. I don't expect you to edit it, I've already sent it. But I thought you'd like to see it."

> My deepest sympathy, Sandra, on your loss of your mother. I remember Kathleen during our college days as so alive and vibrant. She had so many interests and dreams. I'm sure she loved being a mother and loved the special joy of being a grand-mother.
>
> It is a miracle to learn at this moment of loss that there is you, and even more, a grandchild. All miracles are both joyous and terrifying, and I think we will both need some getting used to it, but I would be very grateful to meet you at your very ear-liest convenience. Thank you so much for writing to me and giv-ing me the chance to see you and your daughter.
>
> Love and a thousand blessings,
> Martin

12

PAULINE

An Attorney Struggles with a Biblical Text

Pauline and I became friends many years ago. I had first met her in a political action group to improve the local junior high school, which surprised me because she had no children. Over the years we found ourselves in other community projects: advocacy for new equipment in the school's playground, building a new library, funding the city symphony. I always thought of her as a high-powered lawyer, but I also knew that she was a warm person who was concerned about the community.

One weekend, when my husband was off at his annual professional meeting, Pauline invited me to spend the weekend with her at her country home in Westport, Connecticut. We had no sooner arrived at her elegant house on Friday afternoon and lit a cozy fire in the fireplace when a fierce blizzard began. The electricity was still working, the refrigerator was well stocked, and the snowstorm just intensified our sense of being cut off from all worldly considerations. Over dinner, Pauline opened up and told me:

> The problem is not that I'm not good at what I do; in fact, I've been very successful. I've worked mostly for banks, and, as Willie Sutton famously remarked when asked why he robbed

banks, "That's where the money is." But I'm beginning to wonder if this is all there is, and the woman I sit next to in shul told
me you had really helped a friend of hers find her way. Well,
that's what I need—to find my way.

We set up our schedule for the weekend. I had brought with me
the well-worn Psalter from which I have been reading six psalms a
day for many years, a half-dozen CDs of medieval and Renaissance
music, and a copy of Jo Milgrom's wonderful book *Handmade
Midrash*. She had brought copies of the psalms and *Handmade
Midrash* as well and also furnished a supply of oil pastels—because,
as she told me, she believed that nearly every problem can be solved
by filling pages and pages with color. Very unlawyerlike, I thought,
but nice.

Pauline volunteered to make dinner that night, an arrangement I
happily agreed to. We ate a lip-smacking meal consisting of an endive
salad, grilled salmon with a sauce she whipped up (made from her
own recipe), delicious crunchy asparagus, tiny boiled potatoes, and a
pudding for dessert that could challenge any I've ever had.

We decided to use the time after supper to try out *Handmade
Midrash*. Pauline chose the text of the *Akeidah*—the Binding of
Isaac—in which Abraham is instructed by God to take his son, Isaac,
to Mount Moriah and offer him up as a sacrifice. But after Abraham
prepares an altar and just as he is about to kill his son, he is ordered
by God to stop. He then spots a ram behind him, caught in a thicket
by its horns, and offers it up instead. I read aloud the instructions from
Handmade Midrash, which say to read the biblical text closely and
then cut out different forms in different colors, in this case, one each
to represent Abraham, Isaac, the ram, the altar, and God's presence,
and paste them down in relation to one another. Without first discussing the text, we both busied ourselves with cutting and pasting,
until we agreed that we were done. Pauline then explained that she
had chosen this text because it had troubled her since early childhood.
The story of her relationship with this text unfolded slowly over the
course of that evening in the quiet of her home, surrounded by snow:

I recall the day I made a watercolor of my uncle's resort camp in western Connecticut—actually, the back of the camp, which was normally closed to guests. This was the area around the huge dumpster for all the camp's garbage (I had to make my peace with the odor before I could settle in to draw). Situated nearby were a machine shop, a furniture repair workshop, storage rooms for furniture and equipment, and some mysterious rooms with windows painted black from the inside or boarded up altogether. After wondering if any rats would be attracted to the garbage, I finally settled down, got beyond the odor and the fear, and let the scene reveal itself to me. And to my surprise, I saw beauty in the ramshackle buildings and even in the design of the dumpster (if not in its contents). I realized that I had let fear, disgust, impatience, and prior assumptions conspire to color my view of the area.

These same factors now block my understanding of the *Akeidah* story. I want to approach the biblical text as I did the back of the camp, that is, try to remove those aspects that keep me from letting the story reveal its own deepest nature. I came up with the idea that—to my mind, at least—the *Akeidah* underlies most of the other biblical stories. Once we have read that passage, all others that concern human relationships to God play out against its haunting accompaniment. Here the founder of our faith is ready to sacrifice his beloved—and only—son. As I worked on this "handmade midrash," I told myself to forget all the stories that follow, forget all the commentaries, and forget all the to-do about the story in the High Holy Day liturgy. I told myself to just sit quietly and perhaps the silent, static text will reveal the peripheral voices, the hidden characters, the essential beauty. I thought about that day in the back of the camp. As I sat there with my drawing pad, I heard the sound of the pump turning over in the well. I could distinguish the chemical smell of the water purifier and the sickeningly sweet smell of rotting fruit. As the different odors identified themselves (oil, something burnt), the disgust eased. Perhaps the same thing could happen with the *Akeidah*.

I was struck by Pauline's handmade midrash: there was a clear altar, a stooped Abraham, a trail heading away from the altar—but no Isaac. She commented on the trail heading away from the altar: the steps leading up the mountain were not the same as the steps leading down. She refused to discuss the absence of Isaac. Her disgust was palpable, as was her need to find something redemptive in this foundational text. I wondered about her personal engagement with the story but contented myself with suggesting that she take the *Akeidah*, with the idea of the daily renewal of creation, and relate it to a statement by Bahya ibn Paquda in *Duties of the Heart*, the gist of which is: when people contemplate how they emerged from nonexistence into existence, or from nothing into reality, not because they did anything to merit it but because of God's goodness and grace, they will realize that they are under an obligation to their Creator.

I kept my own commentary on the *Akeidah* to myself because I wanted this to be clearly her evening, and her story addressed some major concern about herself. The chill I felt that night had little to do with the storm outside. I knew Pauline had been using the text to get at an issue of great import, but I was not at all certain whether she would take it further.

On Shabbat morning it was very gray outside (I told Pauline to pull up the shades and let the dark in). We read the psalms we had picked out, discussed them for a while, and then ate a hearty breakfast—juice, scrambled eggs, kosher (soy) bacon, toast, and hot chocolate—slightly more than my usual toast and decaf coffee. Then we had scheduled in two hours of silence, so Pauline settled down to her computer and I helped myself to her oil pastels, which I found very much to my liking. The sun miraculously broke through shortly after lunch, and we agreed that it was the best time to dig out the cars. Digging out the car, which is always a trial and frustration in the city, turned out to be great fun in Pauline's driveway. The snow was glistening white and incredibly soft. Also, it felt good, after all that talking and reflection, to just throw ourselves into strenuous physical activity. When the last windshield was swept clean, we hurried back into the house to warm up and resume our retreat. Pauline gave me a printout of the work she had been doing during my oil pastel session and disappeared. The printout was a letter addressed to herself, recounting what she had been thinking about since the previous night. She listed five statements:

1. I am called.
2. The call is not to a job, but to a commitment that can be lived out in a number of ways.
3. My task is not so much to do as to be.
4. A sense of comfort and contentment will prove that I am on the right path.
5. This comfort does not result from being on automatic pilot; it results from a feeling of God's presence in and through what I am doing.

I was reflecting on whether or not to address each of these points directly when my nose led me to the kitchen. Pauline was just taking a tray of brownies out of the oven. Over a lunch of brownies and milk, we sat in the snug kitchen and briefly touched on her five points. We spent the afternoon sitting in the living room lost in our own thoughts, while listening to Anonymous Four, the Boston Camerata, and other groups performing contemplative medieval and Renaissance music.

Saturday evening it was my turn to prepare dinner, so I heated up some gourmet canned soup on the stove, zapped some precooked barbecued chicken in the microwave, warmed up some bread in the oven, and made some mashed potatoes by mixing instant potato flakes and hot water in a bowl. I gave up cooking long ago. (As my friend, Cathy Bao Bean, explained, "Cooked meals are like the eggs in your ovaries: you're given a supply at birth, and when those are used up, that's it!")

After dinner, we did another round of handmade midrash. By some unspoken agreement, we did not return to the *Akeidah*, but focused instead on *Lech L'cha*, in which Abraham is called to leave his home in Haran and go off to a land that God will show him. I thought that portion would tie in with Pauline's five points in the letter she had shown me. Blue construction paper served as the background of Pauline's collage, and the colors were altogether brighter than her *Akeidah* colors. Her shapes were less definable than the earlier ones, so I simply sat in silence while she explained her work to me: "When I think about Abraham being called, I see him as the first of many. We are each called, although we might not want to acknowledge that. I think you can see by the blocks of color that I'm raising all sorts of questions about the call."

I could see no such thing, but I was willing to hear what she would say next:

> How does Abraham, and how do I, have to be changed in order to answer a new call? What is uncomfortable for him in Haran and for me in my present life? Does Abraham have any minimal requirements for following the call? Do I have any? Is Abraham's life any better after he receives the call but before he answers it? If so, does the difference enable him to discern where the call will take him? I guess the text doesn't really allow me to raise that question, but I'm raising it for myself, not for Abraham.

Handmade Midrash had opened up a discussion that went on until late in the night.

On Sunday morning, after reading psalms and devouring another one of Pauline's hearty breakfasts, we took two more hours of silence. I found my way up to the attic and sat down on a pillow in one corner. At the top of the inverted V of the ceiling hung a small bat, which Pauline had told me took up residence there the previous winter. She had named it Batrick and considered it a friend. Apparently it flew out in the evening through a hole under the attic ceiling and ate every insect that dared to enter the yard. Having slept just six hours the night before, I was beginning to doze off when Pauline called from downstairs that we ought to pack so we could drive home before dark. We agreed that enough material had been raised in these two days to provide us with years of discussion.

Pauline and I continued to see each other after that wonderful weekend, but we agreed that our subsequent discussions would take place within the formal structure of spiritual guidance. I did not refer back to our weekend together, and so I was relieved and delighted that she returned again to the Binding of Isaac, and over the course of the next few months the following interpretation emerged:

> To really think about the Binding of Isaac, I have to think about sacrifice. I believe that the ritual held on historically as long as it did because the worshiper could identify with the sacrificial offering: for Abraham, giving up his son was a way of offering a part of himself to God. The usual offering, of course, was an animal, such as a sheep or a goat. I suppose the best analogy in today's world would be to sacrifice our pet cats or dogs, the animals we've raised, cared for, favored, loved—the animals who trust us. I don't care for the biblical interpretation of the *Akeidah*: that Abraham was being tested and passed the test by his blind obedience to God. I'm also not convinced by any of the more modern interpretations: that he was indeed being tested but flunked the test; that this is an example of infanticide, a practice that the Bible wants us to see in all its "gory" and thereby give up because it so offends us; or that Isaac is sacrificed, is resurrected, and is sacrificed a second time—there really is a midrash that says that!
>
> I want to get to the heart of sacrifice itself. I've thought about that quotation you dropped on me: "When people contemplate how they emerged from nothing, they will realize they are under an obligation to their Creator." Nothingness feels like an important element, if you can call it that.

I remarked that in my experience, every genuine question was also a personal one, but Pauline, while offering a confirming smile, would not elaborate. A month later, she was ready to take the issue of "nothing" further:

From Abraham's point of view, sacrificing Isaac would be entering into Nothing, in the sense that the death of his only biological offspring would end his family line. How, then, could his offspring become as numerous as the stars in the sky, as God had promised him? Only if "offspring" is defined differently—not as his physical descendants but as his spiritual heirs. The numerous offspring, then, would be people whose faith rested in the God of Abraham, who created the world out of Nothing.

We agreed that the *Akeidah*, finally, is the story of a return from Nothing and how that journey leaves us all transformed. We tend to have an image of our self and defend it with a fury. It may be based on our physical appearance, so we might dye our hair or go on diets to retain some idealized self-image; or it may be based on our profession, and we might simply fall apart when we retire; or it could be based on our intellectual prowess, and we find ourselves panicking when we forget names or words. But this self we are defending is not our most authentic self, and when we release it and stop buttressing the walls, we can discover that the walls were not our defense but our prison.

Pauline picked up the discussion again:

> I know just what you mean about self-image. Two years ago, around the time of the symphony benefit, I had a bout with cancer—I don't think you knew about it then. I'm okay now—or, at least, so the doctors assure me—but that was when I first touched on or was touched by Nothingness. My self-image as a strong, healthy person was shattered, yet I knew I was so much more than this body that the doctors were operating on.

She shook her head as if to rid it of an unpleasant image. It was clear to me that the cancer had been a profound experience but I commented that our aim was to help her grow in her relationship with God. She still had not said why she was so drawn to the story of the *Akeidah*, but its powerful elements of Isaac's fear and Abraham's tension suggested that her own journey into this text was anything but impersonal. I suggested that she was far from done with her work on this text.

It all followed rather quickly after that. Two weeks later she went on as if our conversation had never been interrupted:

> The story of the *Akeidah* is the story of the move from determinism to freedom. The story is usually understood from Abraham's point of view: for example, what did it mean for him to be asked to sacrifice his son? But if we look at the story from Isaac's perspective, we recognize that the story allows Isaac to be *more* than Abraham's son. He is even more than what others —his father, especially—do to him. During his journey toward oblivion, he discovers an identity that is deeper than being Abraham's son or even Abraham's disciple. He experiences the Nothing underlying all somethings. It is this experience that is meant to become available to later generations through the rite of sacrifice.

I told Pauline how fascinating I found her interpretations, but that my own questions were different: Where was God in her process of thinking about this text? How was she feeling about Abraham and even about the whole Abrahamic tradition? She laughed, but by now I knew she laughed when she was embarrassed. She made no move to answer my questions, so I decided to outwait her. Finally, she said I was right, it was not simply an intellectual exercise, it was a test. The *Akeidah* may have been God's test of Abraham, but this passage has been her personal test of whether she can fully trust God:

> This story has always blocked my trust. When I was little, one Chanukah I was given a children's Bible with magnificent etchings in it. I don't know the name of the artist, but I've never forgotten the etching that depicted the Binding of Isaac. I said that the story reminded me of the revolting odor at the back of the camp. Well, that etching reminded me of all the terrors in my

childhood nightmares. This huge, monumental man with a long flowing beard, garbed in robes, stood with knife poised over a half-naked boy. I can't sort out whether my terror was due to my own father and his fierceness, or over my "heavenly father" and what would be required of me if I truly wanted to live a spiritual life.

Why had the *Akeidah* become the story she used to test God's trustworthiness? What was her current image of God? Our God-images are formed in childhood, when we think of God as parent, teacher, and police officer all rolled into one. Too often, people carry this primitive conception right into adulthood and old age, instead of modifying it constantly or even replacing it entirely as they mature and gain life experiences.

I assumed that Pauline was shaping her God-image around the time when she received the children's Bible with the terrifying etching and reshaping it when she made the watercolor at the camp. But those two images probably grew out of feelings she already had about the trustworthiness of significant adults in her life and of life itself. We learn to love, to fear, to trust, and to challenge God through the interactions we have with our own family of origin. Although I had known Pauline casually for more than seven years, I knew very little about her family. I knew that she had a sister who lived in a different state, that her father was dead, and that she was somewhat estranged from her mother. From time to time, she hinted about early romances, but she had never married.

I have a one-track agenda, and it is to facilitate a guidee's relationship with God. I have no pretensions about being psychologically astute, but I felt sure that Pauline's relationship with God could blossom only after she had dealt with the fearsome aspects of her parents. With some misgivings, I let Pauline's questions about the *Akeidah* remain on the academic level, but I was listening hard for the story behind the story.

Over the next few meetings, the *Akeidah* issue remained on the table, but Pauline approached it only indirectly. She admitted that she had found a little "wiggle room" by reframing her question in terms of the Nothing, and she harked back to the Ibn Paquda quotation I put forward when we did handmade midrash. Her own drawing of the *Akeidah* with the empty altar also fed into her *Akeidah* mystery. Pauline reflected endlessly on both the *Akeidah* and the sacrificial cult of the Temple and kept returning to Nothing.

One day, Pauline came to my office and remarked on how empty the streets seemed to her. I remarked that I hadn't noticed but that I thought it was a curious way to begin our conversation instead of plunging right in, as she usually did. I had barely gotten the words out when she plunged right into a discussion of the empty altar she had depicted in her handmade midrash. She then spoke in terms of what emptiness meant to her:

> I can describe emptiness in terms of the desert, but my subtext is really my own inner emptiness. I want to preserve that space within myself, because it's what gives me room to grow. I may become uncomfortable with unresolved matters, but it is the unfilled, the unsettled, and the open spaces that are my Holy of Holies.

I knew all of her theoretical talk was intensely personal and practical, so I asked her to describe the God of the *Akeidah*.

"Well, that's hard," she said.

> I don't have a single picture of the God of the *Akeidah*. It's as if there is more than one story going on, or more than one authorial voice. There is the God who puts Abraham to the test—that's the God I fear and try to hide from.

"Is that what you were doing when you went to the back of the camp?" I asked.

"Hiding? Yes, I suppose I was. And I guess it was the terror I brought with me rather than what I discovered there that made that place so frightening."

"You weren't hiding from God?"
"No," she said,

> but one of the images of God in the psalms describes what I was dealing with. In Psalm 139 it says, "Where can I escape from Your spirit? Where can I flee from Your presence?" I was always looking for a hiding place, a safe place, a place I could just quietly be, and not be bothered or hurt.

"From whom were you hiding?"

> My father was fierce, and my mother never protected me. I was the firstborn, so I was supposed to be the good one. My sister would probably give you a very different picture of my father, but to me he was ruler, judge, and executioner.

"And the *Akeidah* gives you a similar image?"
"Only the first part. In the end, it is God who stops Abraham from harming Isaac."
"And was there a voice from God that saved you as well?" I asked.

> I never put it that way to myself before, but maybe. When I was eleven, my father had a heart attack. I didn't wish it, I certainly wanted him to recover, and he did, but he was never as formidable again.

"What did that mean for you?"

> I stopped looking for hiding places and I didn't want to be invisible. I was getting older and stronger, and I guess I was getting ready to challenge him—sort of like Jacob wrestling with God.

"And your view of God?"
"I'm not sure that kept up with the change in my relationship with my father."

There was a lot for Pauline to process in the weeks leading up to our next visit. I tried to read her expression as she entered my office. She seemed energetic, and I just waited to see what would unfold. As usual, she started right in:

> I've always thought of myself as somewhat timorous. I knew my colleagues thought of me as undaunted, even courageous, but it took some of your questions to me last time to really get me to reflect on how my well-disguised fears—my deep, reined-in panic—resulted from a childhood reality and not the present situation. Working through my fears around the *Akeidah* made me conscious of what was holding me back and helped me recognize the call as an invitation, not a prison sentence. Now I see it as a gift, a blessing. I recalled the old joke, "I know we're the Chosen People. But couldn't You choose someone else for a while?" I didn't get what makes chosenness more than an obligation, sometimes even a burden. But now I know. To fully accept our calling is the deepest joy. Sure it's terrifying, but it's also genuinely exciting, and I'm not going to let anything hold me back.

She was racing ahead of me, and I had no idea what she meant by "my call." So I asked her. She immediately began: "I've found what this has all been leading to: I'm going to prepare for ordination."

I shut off my own thinking that wanted to gallop ahead into questions about her many years of preparing for and being an attorney, her relatively advanced age (most seminarians are in their twenties or early thirties), and a host of other matters, but I said nothing and listened as she explained how this decision had come about:

> The expression "growing edge" refers to the part of me that is most alive—the part that is still able to reach out and transform. My growing edge has suddenly taken a new direction. I realized that "more" should not be merely additional instances of what had come before, but a truly new dimension of the world. Instead of quantity, I want to pursue quality.

Here she paused dramatically, ready to reveal the key to all her thinking about Nothing:

> "Nothing" is the means by which I approached the "more." It has been months since I've wrestled with the story of the Binding of Isaac. Finally, I did not simply overcome my disgust for the story or my fear of what Judaism demands of its most serious adherents. After Nothing, I discovered a transformed sense of surrender. Suddenly, I saw "let yourself go" as an expression of surrender. I need to be open to the difficult, but I also must be open to the joyous. In thinking about all this I've even come up with a new quotation to add to your collection. It's from *Markings*, by Dag Hammerskjold: "Self-surrender has been the way to self-realization."

"Pauline," I said, "you've made a very significant decision. May I ask a few questions?"

She replied:

> I'll bet I can anticipate your questions. When I left you last month, we had been discussing my family and how those relationships influenced my God-image. I could hardly believe that my childhood fear of my father could be holding me back from my lifelong desire. But I've done a lot of thinking about my family this past month. It wasn't easy. I had to grow up early. My mother was an alcoholic—I can't believe I actually said that out loud; I never have before. Alcoholism is a big family secret, but perhaps it's even bigger in a Jewish family, where no one is supposed to drink. You probably thought that given my fear of my father, that he was the drunk. No, he was just completely worn out trying to be both father and mother and wage earner for the family. I was supposed to take care of my sister, Lily, who was two years younger than I. I don't recall consciously resenting it, but I must have. Lily went to an out-of-state college—I had stayed in-state so that I could still be available to help her dur-

ing her last two years of high school—and she never returned home.

Three years after her graduation, Lily phoned to tell me that she was getting married. She was running the wedding herself because the groom wasn't Jewish and she was not going to deal with our father's disappointment. The whole time I was on the phone with her, I was staring at a beautiful enamel tile I had attached somewhat crookedly to my wall. When I got off the phone, I decided to straighten the tile, but when it wouldn't come off the wall easily I tried to force it and broke it. I'm now sure I broke it on purpose, because that tile would forever have reminded me of her announcement. I told myself I was glad I would no longer be responsible for Lily, but my own failed relationships haunted me.

Pauline shifted in her seat, sighed heavily, and continued:

My parents showed up for Lily's wedding, but I had no idea whom to sit with. I felt—you know, it's funny: with all the literature I'd read on so many levels, the analogy that came to mind was from "The Farmer in the Dell": "The cheese stands alone." I felt alone, and I felt cheesy. Two years later, my father died. The family reassembled for the funeral, but we haven't all been together again since then, and that's close to fifteen years. I finished my law degree a year later, and there was no one I could really share that with.

"And your mother?"

This is really amazing: she stopped drinking! An aunt sent me a clipping that my mother was running for school board. This is the woman who never attended a single PTA meeting in my entire childhood. Again, I felt as I had with Lily: relieved that I wouldn't have to be responsible for her. Even so, I had no desire to reinsert myself in the family.

I threw myself into lawyering, and at first I loved it. But something was missing—I guess you'd say this is part of the God-image thing. However frightening my father's scrutiny was, it was an indication of his caring. But at this point in my life, I feel no one cares, except I don't know what I would have done without the synagogue community. I began taking courses through the synagogue. I guess after I had the cancer scare—I told you about that.

I nodded, and she went on:

That really shook me up. I was determined not to die before I had lived. My doctor said I had a cancerous growth. I said I had cancer. The difference was that she saw what I had as a small, self-contained incident, and once it was treated, she said I had a long life ahead of me. But I see it as a daily reminder that I don't have forever to live. Somewhere inside I've always known what I was called to, but I've been afraid to pursue it. But now I'm determined. Being a rabbi is what I was born to do.

"Could we return to the *Akeidah*?" I asked. "You told me there were many different Gods in the story, different authorial voices. Now that you are about to make this commitment, who is God for you?"

"God is not the one who tests Abraham," she said. "I know that— and I know that because I know God."

Pauline's voice had taken on a gentle tone I hadn't heard from her before. She said:

I was never afraid of God, I was afraid of my father. The God who said to Abraham, "Do not harm the lad," was the God I knew. As I ran and hid, as I trembled in my bed at night, that was who was there for me, who comforted me, who guided me. Going for ordination is not my payback to the God who protected me, it is a joyous response to the invitation to use all my gifts.

Was this really the right decision for her? I saw a tough road ahead—five years of being a student again, of being in a very subordinate position. But I also saw a determination to see it through. She is now in her fourth year of seminary and is doing really well. She is interning at a temple with a rabbi who absolutely loves her. But more important, she is thrilled to be doing "God's work," as she mockingly refers to her position, and she feels that for the first time in her life, she is doing what she was called to do.

13

SARAH

A Marriage and the Healing of Childhood Losses

I saw Sarah over a period of five years, during which we explored her ideas about marriage, her fears of betrayal, her need to trust, and her desire to forge a new sense of herself. I regarded her as a model for the varieties of love, forgiveness, and healing.

Sarah was an intelligent woman in her forties who looked younger than her years. She wore no makeup, nor did she need any. Her richly colored dark brown hair, dark eyebrows, luminous brown eyes, and full red lips defined a face that drew one to want to get to know her. Dare I say she projected both beauty and brains?

The original impetus for her asking to speak with me was her husband's confession of infidelity. They had a history of trying to nip any marriage problems in the bud. She and Fred had seen a marriage counselor twice before during their twenty years together, and they were both satisfied that the short-term counseling helped them through some tough times. But, she said, she sensed a need now to seek out what her religion might have to offer. She chose spiritual guidance rather than pastoral counseling because she thought a rabbi might be unsympathetic to some of her unorthodox ideas about Judaism. The questions she was posing, she thought, were quite different from those she was struggling with earlier, in that they dealt with her view of herself and what she called her religious beliefs, rather than her relationship to Fred. Nevertheless, her opening words expressed her hurt at Fred's betrayal, as she put it:

> I know that Fred is better than anyone else I might meet. I even know that he is essentially a very good person. But I feel— wounded, shamed, rejected, criticized in an unanswerable but intimate way.

When something traumatic happens in a person's family—a child's death, a partner's infidelity, a parents' divorce—the affected family member usually feels somehow responsible: "It all happened because of what I did (or failed to do)." It is common knowledge that children of divorce are likely to believe that they caused their parents' breakup, but spouses of unfaithful partners are just as likely to believe that they caused their spouse's behavior. The reasoning is simple: "If I'd been good enough, my spouse would not have 'strayed.'" It would actually take more than a year before Sarah could begin to look at the reasons for Fred's infidelity. Her more immediate problem was a deeply wounded sense of self.

Instead of going into her relationship with Fred, I asked Sarah about her prayer life, which she described in terms of form rather than content. She told me about the prayers she recited, not the feelings they aroused. Clearly, there was an essential question she wasn't articulating, and I guessed that it was whether she could trust God enough to let her live more fully and honestly. She had never been truly intimate with Fred, fully open with her children, completely engaged with her work, or emotionally involved with her synagogue. She was likable and efficient, but always holding back. I suggested that she treat this crisis as a gift in disguise, one that was really meant to heal her emotional wounds, which preceded not only Fred's infidelity, but also preceded her becoming a mother and even her marriage to Fred. They resulted, it turned out, from her father's unending criticism, which began as far back as she could remember.

Somehow, Fred had penetrated Sarah's heavy defenses and convinced her that he really, *really* wanted to marry her, and not, as she first thought, out of pity:

It took many months before I could convince myself that he wanted *me* and not just *anyone*. During my early adolescence, when I was first beginning to date, my father had asked me, "Are you certain it's not just platonic?", not believing that I could possibly be attractive to any boy. Long after his death, I was still hearing that question as if he were there, asking it in the same tone he had used with my first boyfriend. He had often remarked on how my sister, Peggy, could be so buxom and I so flat-chested: "Did we have different fathers?" he liked to ask.

When Fred and I finally did get married, we had a joyous time setting up house, watching silly TV programs together, and getting to know each other's likes and dislikes. We couldn't wait to start a family, and I got pregnant either on our wedding night or a day or two later. Those early years were just great—being out from under my father's control was reason enough to be happy, but Fred did wonders for my ego. He loved and respected me no matter what I did or didn't do, and taking care of our three babies felt like a reward I didn't deserve.

Now fast-forward to six months ago. I knew Fred was less than happy with his work—he's an electrical engineer—but when I considered, as I often did, how comfortable we were, how the kids had all gone to good schools, and how we had both worked hard to become financially well-off, I decided that I had done all I could do for the marriage. I was deeply shocked when he told me he had had an affair. I thought, perhaps I wasn't sexy enough for him anymore, or maybe he had cravings I couldn't fulfill.

We agreed to go for marriage counseling again, but I got furious when the therapist started focusing on *my* emotional distance—I was, after all, the wronged party. But secretly I recognized some truth in what the counselor said, and I made an effort to relate better to Fred. Things improved, up to a point.

At the counselor's suggestion, I went for individual therapy, and while I did discuss some of my childhood problems, I somehow never got to the ongoing question: can I still trust God? I might have settled for the healed relationship with Fred and left it at that, but the question would not go away.

At High Holy Day services I felt myself choking up—during *Yizkor*, the prayer for remembering the dead, I began to cry as I remembered my father—and finally had to leave services because I couldn't stop crying. That was three weeks ago, and the experience was so unnerving that I knew I had to do something about it. I felt tears welling up at odd moments during the day. Maybe I just need an antidepressant.

I reminded her that I'm not a psychopharmacologist and asked her just why she thought I was the right person for her to see. "Well, since my crying jags started during *Yizkor*," she said, "I thought that I must have a religious problem."

We began by talking about what happened at *Yizkor*. She was embarrassed that she had cried. There were people in the congregation who were newly bereaved. Why, she thought, should she cry, when her father had been dead for twenty-eight years? I asked if she had cried at the time he died. She couldn't remember, but she described the events surrounding his death:

The summer after graduating from college, I worked with the understanding that my girlfriend June and I would do the grand tour of Europe, after the tourist season so our money would go further. Two weeks into the trip, I got a wire at American Express that my father had had a heart attack. I flew home, but although I saw my father, I wasn't sure he even knew I was there. He lay in a semi-comatose state for ten days. When he died, I went on automatic pilot. I can't even remember how the arrangements were made for the funeral, breaking up the house—I suppose Peggy did most of it. June came back with me from Europe, but I lost touch with her after that—I don't remember how come. I met Fred three years later. He was young, handsome, intelligent, and very gentle. I guess I was cold and aloof—which Fred interpreted as shy.

"Where was God in all of this?" I asked.

"Well, God was clearly present when I became a mother," she replied. "My daughter was beautiful, even when she was all red and screaming. I just love her completely and unreservedly."

Was God also present at her father's death? Suddenly the evenly pitched story stopped. Sarah shifted about uneasily in her chair. When at last she spoke, she remarked: "I know God was present as I was coming home from the funeral, but I didn't know what to do about it. It was twenty-eight years ago—I can't remember."

I didn't say anything. She stared at me for a long while. Eventually I said, "You know, you're withdrawing."

She started to speak, stopped herself, started and stopped herself again, then finally said:

> Religion was something my father and I did together. We would often go to services together on Friday night, just the two of us. I guess my mother and Peggy were cooking. My Dad was really religious, and he insisted that I play an active role in the synagogue. I'd been active in Hillel in college, and he was glad about that. But after he died—

She didn't finish the sentence; she just blurted out, "It wasn't fair!"

"You were very angry at God," I said.

"How could I be angry at God?" was her reply.

"Well, here is this good man who cared for you, and now he dies."

"Yes," she agreed, "and God shows up as if I'm supposed to feel all pious, when what I felt was—"

As we both waited expectantly to see what she would say, I heard some custodians outside my door, speaking loudly about measuring "the goddam f——g door frame." I wondered whether Sarah would use the interruption as an excuse to change the subject to something more comfortable. In a way, she did: "I did all the right things," she said. "I showed up at services every day for a year to say *Kaddish*."

I decided not to let her off the hook: "And what you felt was—?"

"Angry at God—but that's so scary!"

I said that anger was part of any genuine relationship.

"But I never get angry," she said.

My face said it all.

"Oh," she said, "you think I've never been in a genuine relationship."

I asked whether she had been angry at either Fred or the woman with whom he'd had the affair. No, she said, she was just hurt.

Was she ever angry at her sister?

> No, quite the reverse. Peggy has had it in for me practically since I was born. For five years she was an only child, and then along comes this cute new baby. And, a few years later, she was forced to share a room with me. She never missed a chance to be mean to me or to belittle me. Of course, she was my older sister, so whatever she said must have been true, I thought. But I was never mad at her.

"How could you not be?" I asked. "Anger is an important emotion, even if some people train themselves to avoid it."

Obviously I hit a raw nerve—not that she became visibly angry, but her voice betrayed controlled emotion: "Anger drives people away," she said. "I make it a point never to get angry at work. And Fred and I could heal our earlier marriage problems because I didn't get mad. You know, I felt like a regular Job when I lost my father and then my sister moved away."

"Job got angry," I said, straining to keep my answers soft. "Look at some of his speeches!"

"But they always talk about the *patience* of Job," she countered.

"Who are 'they'? Read the text for yourself."

Suddenly, she smiled. "Is this a homework assignment?"

I nodded. She picked up her things and opened the door to leave. The custodians were still outside in the hall, measuring other doors, and then hastily measuring their language when they realized we were within earshot.

Sarah started our next meeting by saying that she had nothing to talk about. OK, I said, then let me quote something from my favorite rebbe, William Blake. She always laughed when I introduced poets or novelists as if they were rabbis. But she was also interested in hearing the quotation:

> We are put on earth, a little space
> That we may learn to bear the beams of love.

Sarah sat quietly for a very long time—a minute of silence in the middle of a conversation feels like an eternity—and then slowly began to "unpack" the meanings she saw in those words: "'Bear the beams of love' might mean to carry the love. It makes it seem as though love is a burden."

"Is it?" I asked.

When I was young I used to think that the greatest thing was to be loved. I didn't see that it carried responsibility with it. Later, in my teens, a guy I didn't particularly like told me that he loved me. That was no fun! And still later I discovered that it really feels better to give than to receive. The more I loved, the more lovable the world became to me. When I loved books by a certain author, I had the greatest fun going to used bookstores and finding her books. When I knew the names of a few birds, what a delight to recognize them sitting on a branch in the morning.

But, yes, it can be a burden to recognize that someone loves you, especially someone who makes demands and has expectations you think you can never fulfill. I'm sure that my father loved me, but his love was difficult for both of us. It certainly wasn't unconditional—does anyone really experience unconditional love, or is it like the happily ever after in fairy tales? My father's love was totally conditional, and I could never meet the conditions. I was furious that he wanted me to be someone I wasn't, but I couldn't hate him—because I loved him.

"The person we love," I said, "is very often the person we hate, because that's who can hurt us the most."

Sarah refused to acknowledge that she heard what I said and instead plunged ahead:

> "To bear the beams of love" can also mean to discover that we have been loved. I tried that exercise you suggested in one of our sessions—recalling all the people who have loved me and contributed to my becoming who I am. I thought about my aunt Molly, who once baked me chocolate chip cookies after I had exclaimed over the cookies she served when we visited her. Then there was Julia, my best friend in high school, who was willing to hear all my dramas—and could keep a secret. And, oh yes, my Hillel director, who suggested that I run for office at Hillel. As my list grew longer and longer, I realized that there has been a tremendous amount of love all around me. I know—you want me to see God's love in and through all this, but I'm not ready yet.
>
> And I guess there is a third meaning of "to bear the beams of love": to generate, give birth to, love. That's really true. After Lois was born, I was deliriously happy, I loved everyone, and I even felt like getting closer to my sister. It just suddenly dawned on me that she's a good person, and I was so overwhelmed with love, I wanted to express it in every possible way. So, before I even got home from the hospital, I dropped her a note and said how glad I was that Lois would have her for an aunt. It didn't end all my problems with my sister, but I did experience how a deep sense of love makes you want to spread it around.

"So when you can't love, or spread love, it might be because you feel threatened in some way, or don't feel loved yourself," I ventured.

"If I knew," she said, "if I really knew I were loved in some absolute way, I could slow down, loosen up, and feel that the whole world wasn't directed against me."

I asked Sarah if we could get back to her sister for a moment. "What did you have in mind when you dropped her that note?"

"I was saying that I loved her, and I guess I was trying to let her know indirectly that I forgave her for torturing me all the years I was growing up."

"Had she expressed regret at all the misery she had visited on you? Is that what made you want to forgive her?"

Sarah said that her sister was not at all repentant, that they had never even talked about the past.

"But you forgave her anyway," I noted. "Can you explain how you were able to do that?"

"I don't know—I just felt so full, so joyous, so overflowing with love."

"And you felt safe?" At this point, I could imagine Perry Mason jumping up and saying that I was "leading the witness."

"Yes," she said, "I felt completely safe, that nothing could possibly hurt me."

"So your feelings of safety and love allowed you to forgive your sister. And did you forgive Fred as well?" I asked.

"No," she answered quickly.

> I guess I haven't really forgiven Fred. I've agreed not to bring it up again. I get along with him day-to-day, but I'm not open, welcoming, and overflowing with love, the way I was in the days immediately following Lois's birth.

"Is the problem, then, that you don't feel love for Fred or that you don't feel safe?"

"Well," she replied,

> right now I'm back to where I was when I was living at home. I feel completely unlovable, and I'm back to wondering what Fred ever saw in me. And although he really has made me feel more and more valuable and desirable with every passing year, I've internalized so many of my father's criticisms and jibes that

when Fred had the affair, I assumed he was just verifying what my father had been saying all along, that no man would ever really love me. So, to answer your question, I guess I don't feel safe with Fred anymore, since he can hurt me so badly."

"Did you forgive your father?" I asked.

Well, yes. The real breakthrough came when my uncle Willy told me that my grandmother hadn't wanted another son and that she had actually told my father that whenever she got mad at him. I finally realized that all his criticism of me was really a kind of autobiography. Anyway, he's long dead, so he can't hurt me again.

I let Sarah know that I was saying something important by speaking very slowly: "Do you now recognize that you were loved?"

I know that my father always loved me "in his fashion" (apologies to Cole Porter), and I let his "fashion" determine that no one else could possibly love me. But I can now separate out that there were others who let me sense their love—uncles, aunts, teachers, friends.

"And God?"

"I know that from time to time," Sarah said, "but I can't retain it. It's such a powerful thought that it takes exceptional time for me to simply absorb the idea that I am loved."

At this point, I reminded her of the structures of remembrance that we have set up to help us pay attention to the gifts we receive and events we experience. For example, we say blessings to acknowledge the wonders that surround us: the food we eat, the wine we drink, fragrant spices, new clothes, thunder, lightning, rainbows. All of these wonders are gifts of love. A list of the great teachers we had is also a remembrance of gifts of love. And we find that gratitude, like love, is even more wonderful to give than to receive.

About five weeks later, Sarah came in looking more content and open than I had ever seen her. Her eyes sparkled, her mouth was relaxed into a smile. She obviously couldn't wait to tell me, so I asked her what was up.

"A miracle has happened," she said, glowing.

> Fred and I took a weekend together into the country, and he said he knew that my whole life was about learning to trust God. I was shocked and thrilled that he had recognized that. Then he said he hoped that en route to that trust I would also come to trust him. I had never put the two loves together before, but he did it so powerfully and suddenly that it was as if a dam had burst open and all those thoughts and feelings came pouring out. I even got angry, but he wasn't put off by my anger. He saw it, as you had hinted he might, as genuine communication. He told me what he must have told me many times before but that I couldn't really take in then, that the affair had had nothing to do with me. It had to do with his feelings about himself, that he was devastated that it had hurt me, and that he was determined to understand himself better and, he hoped, to regain my absolute trust.

I didn't have to ask Sarah where God was in all this. She was well ahead of me:

> God's love convinced me that I was lovable. That was what made it possible for me to experience Fred's infidelity as a problem, not a threat. As you pointed out, forgiveness becomes possible when we don't feel threatened and when we are overflowing with love.

14

JOAN
A Young Guidee Returns as a Social Worker

Joan was the youngest guidee I have had so far, and one of the most creative. During the time we met, she changed from focusing on her creations—sketches and drawings—to making sense of her world and her role in creating it.

I first met Joan during the summer following her first year of college. I was living and teaching in Boston at the time, and she was my third or fourth guidee. Her undergraduate experience up till then, at a college in western Massachusetts, had been disappointing, in that it felt to her like an extension of secondary school—except that as a senior in high school she had enjoyed far more freedom. In college, by comparison, her entire freshman-year curriculum was prescribed. She found herself sitting in large classes studying English, third-year French, world history, and math "for poets." She also found herself bringing a sketchbook to class and filling it with drawings of her fellow students and professors, while her note-taking languished. Sandra, Joan's Hillel director and a former student of mine, had come to know her and sensed that there was a larger question lurking behind her unhappiness. But since Joan was going to be spending the summer at her parents' home in Boston, she realized that sending her to the college counseling center wouldn't do any good. She also believed that if Joan didn't get the right guidance, she might become lost to the Jewish community.

Joan could easily have posed for a magazine ad as your typical college student. Fresh-faced, with light brown hair, she wore a pretty smile as comfortably as she fit into her low-cut jeans and artsy, loose-hanging top. When we talked, she looked at me directly with her warm, brown eyes and left no doubt that she was completely engaged. And because her eyes never wandered from mine, I knew I was getting her absolute attention. She had brought the sketchbook with her and soon had pulled it out of her backpack to show to me. I noticed that below each picture was a set of numbers, such as 118:4. I looked through the entire book as she watched my reaction. She then asked me:

"Do you know what, like, the numbers stand for?"

It was important to her that I know. I thought, ah, I'm being tested, and felt relieved that I knew the answer. "They identify a psalm number and a verse."

She expressed shock that I could guess her secret code so effortlessly. I couldn't help but ask how she happened to choose this psalm code.

She explained that she always carried a small Book of Psalms with her so she could read from it whenever she had some spare subway or waiting-line time. The edition she showed me was the size of a cell phone. Her backpack, a war surplus flight bag, also contained a Swiss army knife, a sketch pad, a kneaded eraser, several pencils, charcoal, a bottle of spring water, hair implements, small pages torn from a Post-it pad, and a welter of other school and nonschool items.

"As an artist, have you ever tried to illustrate the psalms?" I asked her.

She seemed intrigued, so I extended the question: "The way you are using the psalms to comment on your art, you could just as easily take any text with standard numbering, such as Shakespeare's sonnets or Plato's dialogues. Have you thought of using your art to comment on the psalms, instead of the other way around?"

It seemed important that Joan carried the psalms as part of her daily equipment, and I hoped it would help me reach out to her. Officially I was still in the dark about Joan's reasons for coming to see me, although she did say that she found her classes boring. Like most of the people I guide, Joan had contacted me without offering her "presenting problem." I asked Joan if she thought boredom was reason enough to come for spiritual guidance.

"I guess not. Well, like, if you don't want me to come back, like, I'll totally understand."

(For Joan, a complete sentence needed a noun, a verb, and the word "like" or, occasionally, "totally." To save space and nerves, I've edited out these words in the remainder of this case.) "No," I said, "that was not my intention in asking that. I hoped the question would get you to think about why you're here and to articulate it."

"OK. I've decided that the problem is me. Actually, I'm bored with me, and I think I'm just using my classes so I can blame them for being unhappy."

"Oh," I said, "so you're unhappy, too?"

"Yes, but I'm unhappy with myself," she said,

> because I don't really know where I'm going or even why I'm going. I have a great reverence for life, my own included—but I feel as though I've reached something of a dead end. I need some direction, to find some purpose, I don't know. About the only time I can lose myself is when I'm lost in the psalms—oh, I've always thought that would be a good title for my autobiography: "Lost in the Psalms."

It seemed to me, given her deep involvement with the psalms, that she needed to get clearer about her relationship with God and that, through the psalms, she might be able to explore her ideas about God. Of course, using the psalms as a code would not foster that connection, but entering more fully into the world of the psalms might. Over the next few visits, Joan discovered that the more she dug into the psalms, the more layers of meaning were revealed to her. She figured out, for example, that there is no "happily ever after": no sooner does the biblical David find a resting place for the Ark than he has to contend with enemies.

Joan was not the only one to spend hours with the psalms—writing out the words with a calligraphy pen, drawing illustrations all around the printed text. She even found a book with photographs illustrating the psalms, but she felt that the interpretations were not only too literal, they were also too far removed from the time when the psalms originated. She collected illustrated editions of the psalms, especially those with illuminated initial letters showing flowers, fruit, birds, small mammals, palm trees, and cacti—anything that is described in biblical accounts of the Holy Land. What she said she did find, however, was that none of the artists ever addressed the fury of the Psalmist, even when a verse from the psalm itself sets the stage, as in Psalm 102:7–8: "I am like a great owl in the wilderness . . . I am like a lone bird upon a roof."

She recounted her engagement with that particular psalm:

> All I saw was the usual Middle Eastern flora and fauna, no depiction of the anguish and the loneliness. I quickly opened my sketchbook and began to lay down colors with fury. The psalms were not pretty poems, so I would be as bold with my oil pastels as David was with his words. When I looked up from my drawing, I saw that my fingers were stained from holding the pastels so hard. I actually felt as if I'd been running. I breathed deeply several times and began to notice my surroundings, especially the shadows that now filled the corners of the room. I slowly allowed my glance to return to the page on which I'd been working and took another deep breath. It was there! I really had captured the anger, the fear, the pain. I felt such a rush of energy that I jumped up and down, trying to click my heels together twice before I hit the ground. After around five attempts I was sufficiently calm, so I placed a piece of onionskin over the oil pastel and closed the book.

Out of habit, I began to speak to Joan slowly and softly, as I did whenever I wanted a guidee to pay close attention, but then realized that I didn't need to invoke this trick with her because she *always* paid close attention. I suggested that her need for a picture of abject loneliness was no less literal than a drawing of a bird on a roof, which she found so simpleminded. "The psalm is not just about loneliness," I said, "but about a relationship that underlies light and darkness, good and evil."

Joan's aesthetic sensitivity made her aware of a role for all the elements in a text, so that combining them creates a richer beauty. I used that awareness to help Joan see beyond the manifest content of celebration, petition, confession, praise, and intercession, to the latent content of a relationship that harmonizes all the differing tendencies in human life: "Look at a series of your sketches and tell me what they are saying."

Joan frowned. "You should know better. If I could say it, I wouldn't have to draw it."

I refused that answer: "You know that your drawings are saying something. How can you hope to interpret the psalms if you don't make the same effort in terms of your art?"

She began to flip through her sketchbook. Something I had said and some of her own thoughts began to come together. The psalms don't say just one thing; they say many things at once. Some are complaints, some are expressions of joy, some express remorse, while others convey celebration. Her own sketches displayed the same variety. Those drawn on the campus tended to be cheerful and energetic because, she explained, she was happy when she was outside. But the drawings created surreptitiously in class tended to be more complaining, even upset. And the images formed late at night, when she was alone in her room, often portrayed the world as opposing her. She was not ready yet to say what the drawings meant, but some ideas were germinating. Nor did I know any more than she did; we were figuring this out together.

Our next visit went directly to the psalms. Joan sat down, pulled open her war surplus bag, and took out her Book of Psalms. We had begun with Psalm 73, and Joan said she was genuinely shocked that my interpretation of one passage could differ so completely from hers. Where Joan read Psalm 73:25 ("Whom else have I in heaven? / And having You, I want no one on earth") as a statement of loneliness and isolation, I pointed out that the passage does not read, "Having no one on earth, I take refuge in You." Rather, it says, "Having You, I want no one on earth." I reminded Joan of her own inner life, which was so rewarding that she no longer noticed whether or not she had many friends, or so she had said. Next, Joan emphasized a phrase from verse 26, "My body and mind fail," while I focused on the continuation of that thought, "But God is the stay of my mind, my portion forever." Joan ended our meeting early because she felt she had taken in more than she could process in one session. As a kind of closer, I threw out another line from the same psalm: "As for me, nearness to God is good" (verse 28).

"What does that *mean*?" Joan asked with urgency and exasperation. She remarked that it seemed so close to being understood, but it was just beyond reach.

"You're right," I said. "Time out. These psalms are all addressed to God, but we haven't discussed what 'God' even means." Joan started to protest that she knew, but I continued: "You know how other people have used the title, but until you can discover in your own experience a reason to apply it, it's hard to make real sense of these passages. Every time you see the word 'God,' why don't you just replace it with an X—for unknown. Wait to discover what it means, and then we'll return to Psalm 73. Now go home and rest!"

When I saw Joan again two weeks later, it was on a hot and humid summer day in Boston, with the air-conditioning in my building "temporarily out of service," as the posted notice said. She suggested we take refuge in a nearby soda shop, but I was sure somebody or other would come by and ask to join us. I knew of a hotel a few blocks down Huntington Avenue with an air-conditioned lobby, where I thought we could gain a measure of privacy if we sat off in a corner. Alas, the lobby was filled with people who had had the same idea. We then repaired to the bar lounge, where we found a suitable place and ordered soft drinks, much to the annoyance of the waiter. Although I dislike having any distractions, such as food, during spiritual guidance sessions, I decided under the circumstances to appease the waiter and ordered a cheese-and-crackers appetizer.

When we had finally settled down, Joan said that she recognized how many different ways there are to tell the story behind any of the psalms. The Psalmist is sometimes sad, sometimes joyous, but always alive and passionate. She began her reconstruction of Psalm 45:3: "You are fairer than all men; / your speech is endowed with grace." Joan said that meeting X was like meeting someone who had changed her life in radical ways. She found the appropriate text in Psalm 40:4: "He put a new song into my mouth, / a hymn to our God."

"You know," she said, "when someone likes you and sees something about you that you never saw before, well, then for the first time you can see it yourself and believe it."

And then, with a little hesitancy, she added, from Psalm 139:14, "I praise You, / for I am awesomely, wondrously made." Joan explained, with more hesitancy that barely hid her embarrassment, that she could finally recognize her beauty because someone had loved her— the unknown X of Psalm 45. Joan remembered the first time she had noticed the golden highlights in her own dark brown hair. She used to refer to her hair as "mouse brown," but someone, and even now she blushed furiously when she remembered, had spoken of the hidden sparks of gold within her and illustrated that in terms of the highlights in her hair. Someone had seen in her what she felt her daily acquaintances had not. And at that moment, she accepted this new perspective and quoted from Psalm 139, "I praise You, / for I am awesomely, wondrously made."

She thought that when she told me about the highlights in her hair, I might compliment her or tease her. Rather, I let us both sit in quiet appreciation of that perceptive compliment, which turned out to have come from her boyfriend. And she was clear that she valued it *because* it grew out of a relationship. I tossed her a pencil and asked her to draw her hand, and although puzzled, she was happy to do it. As she followed the contours, she said she could see the wonder that lay in her own hand. External compliments can be taken away, but now her sure, personal knowledge allowed her to say, "for I am awesomely, wondrously made."

I hoped she would recognize that appreciating her own hand was also grounded in a significant relationship, so I asked her, "Suppose you take seriously that the psalms really are 'the scroll recounting what befell the Psalmist'—recounting the Psalmist's life with God. What would that mean?" Joan did not answer right away, and it was clear that her mind was churning. In our first session, she had not really talked about God. To discuss God seriously with another person seemed to her truly difficult, perhaps even impossible. And although I was not like anyone else in that I took her and her art seriously, I wondered whether she could voice what she was thinking and feeling.

I gave her ample time to gather her thoughts, and finally she said, "I have trouble talking about God." I was neither surprised nor concerned.

> I find it easier to talk about my art—but last time, when I told you about the psalm code, you said something about the psalms being a form of worship. I guess I heard you, but I didn't make the connection, that is, I didn't see how thinking of the psalms as worship would help me understand what underlies the psalms.

"How might art be a form of prayer?" I asked.

Joan started to answer in terms of celebration and praise, but then she stopped. She was not some bright student showing how well she could respond. She knew I wanted her to think more deeply. She thought about her own sketchbook. What happened when she walked around the campus, chose a scene, and began to sketch it? The longer and harder she looked, the more she found revealed. She knew—she had always known—that while some people admired her ever-thickening sketchbook, the sketches were only a by-product of a much more significant adventure. She managed to stammer some of this, and I quietly nodded. She was knowing something now in a way she had never known before.

Joan decided it was time for her to say something about all her doubts. She began, "I always think of my sketchbook as 'My Angry Freshman Year.'"

I countered that I had come to think of it as "Psalms: A Journal of Creativity."

Joan started, electrified. "Psalms: A Journal of Creativity," she repeated. "I love that!"

I continued, "The whole book is really about your creative process." I reminded her that when we had talked earlier, it was she who had quoted Psalm 87:7, "Singers and dancers alike will say: / 'All my roots are in You.'" I had asked her about Psalm 107:14, "He brought them out of the deepest darkness, / broke their bonds asunder," and reminded her how literally she had read that. And yet she had felt a similar sense of liberation when her pencil could finally flow again over the paper. How often had she sat before a blank piece of paper as if before an unplowed field? How often, by will alone, had she prepared her tools, readied herself, and begun the process of drawing? And then the paper responded, the drawing blossomed, and she, indeed, could believe Psalm 126:5–6, "They who sow in tears / shall reap with songs of joy. / Though he goes along weeping, / carrying the seed-bag, / he shall come back with songs of joy, / carrying his sheaves."

I saw Joan only three times that summer and intermittently during her final two years of college. Before her and since, I never had a guidee whose spiritual life moved as fast as hers did. (Ah, the nimbleness of the young!) She continued to draw, although she did not major in art. Art was her gift, she reasoned, her way of communicating with herself, not something she wanted to display for teachers and other students to judge. Instead, she chose a joint major in sociology and psychology. I knew that she applied to my college's School of Social Work upon graduation but chose a university in New York State, and then, as is too often the case, I lost touch with her.

It took six years and a move with my husband back to New York City, where we had both grown up, before I saw Joan again. During the intervening years, she had earned a graduate degree in social work and had taken a job with the New York City Bureau of Child Welfare. She called and asked if I remembered who she was and whether I would still be willing to see her. I assured her on both counts and was delighted to reunite with her the following week.

Joan joked that she couldn't understand how she could fall into deadness so young, that she was probably the youngest social worker on record who suffered from burnout. I explained that people often felt burned if they were in the wrong job. She said she was doing useful, effective work, but the old joy was gone. Was it selfish to focus on her own aliveness? she wanted to know. Could there be any value in taking time to reconsider her career? We touched on that question, then simply left it and moved back to more familiar ground.

There was a time in her life when she had never been without sketch pad and pencil. When had she ceased to carry them with her as naturally as she carried her keys? The loss of the sketching was a loss of her voice, of her way of seeing and communicating with the world. She thought of the backpack and its contents, and what stood out in her mind were a sketch pad and her small Book of Psalms. At that time, the psalms had become a vocabulary for thinking through whatever she was experiencing. It had been a rich and subtle palette with which to paint the story of her life. Could it be that again as she faced new questions?

The psalms were certainly full of complaints. She had to admit that even now, she relished the audacity of the Psalmist. Her own creative process, by comparison, felt dry. Maybe there was a clue to that in Psalm 63:2: ". . . as a parched and thirsty land that has no water." I suggested that the gifts that nourished her in the past could sustain her now, that once again she could wander in this land that once fed her creativity. Despite our returning to old ground, I sensed a shyness, an embarrassment. She had last drawn with passion when she was an undergraduate, and maybe, she mused, only undergraduates could go beyond their own inhibitions and portray the intensity of passion. No, she said, there had to be another model. Together we remembered how she had collected both angry psalms and love psalms. I let the first two meetings serve to reconnect us and watched for the familiar sparkle and outspokenness. Unlike the earlier time that I saw her, it took about three meetings before I felt we were really in the present.

Joan was certain that art was a way of thinking, not the way she wanted to earn her livelihood. The longer we talked, the clearer it

became that what she wanted was not a new career but a new relationship to her present career. She expressed gratitude that I never
used the word "hobby" in talking about her art. I find that using the
word "hobby" trivializes people's creative language, almost like asking
what they find to amuse themselves on rainy days. Joan was not looking for amusement; she was trying to find ways to express her deepest insights. Her creativity was in dialogue with the Psalmist's creative
expression, and together we recognized creativity as a profound form
of worship.

The "answers" she arrived at in college no longer held during her
first years of work. The Bureau of Child Welfare had many of the same
risks as the trauma unit of a hospital—you see a great amount of suffering, but despite your best efforts, you can ameliorate very little.
What chances, really, did her young clients have of ever realizing a fully
human life? They began with lives of abandonment and abuse. Long
before they could develop essential trust, they had already experienced
a lifetime of neglect and even brutality. As I talked with Joan over the
ensuing months, she recognized that she was trying to learn where she
could find room for hope. Could her little clients be free from fear and
abuse? Could they be free to find meaning and make choices? What
was freedom anyway—was it a given or an achievement? To what
extent was her own freedom simply the luck of the draw?

I asked her if the world was more horrible than it had been in the
days of King David.

> No, but David tended to focus on the soldiers and those who
> consented to go to war. If a woman had written the psalms, she
> would have raised questions about the fatherless children, those
> without food.

Joan had raised an important challenge about the perspective of
the Psalmist, so we agreed to examine the psalms carefully and try
to spell out the elements in this biblical world that might apply to
the Bureau of Child Welfare. Could the BCW be conceived of in
that framework—psalms of a just God viewing victims with many

enemies? I enjoyed preparing for my next meeting with Joan, but I was determined to wait for whatever she would present and not rush in with my own views.

Joan came in and handed me a short list of quotations from psalms:

"Whoever fears *Adonai* will be shown what path to choose." (Psalm 25:12)
"See I will bring a scroll recounting what befell me." (Psalm 40:8)
"I trust in the faithfulness of God forever and ever." (Psalm 52:10)
"But God is the stay of my mind, my portion forever." (Psalm 73:26)

"Great," I said, "and what do these psalms mean to you, and how do they apply to the actual world of the BCW?"

She then began her commentary on the four verses she had carefully chosen.

> That first verse, "Whoever fears *Adonai* will be shown what path to choose": I used to believe that—in fact, I still believe it, except when I'm actually dealing with my clients. I want to believe that they have choices, but they have been beaten down so often and at such tender ages that I fear they may have lost any possibility of exercising choice. But I can't have a divided theology, one for my own privileged status and one for the workplace. Somehow the God who has always guided me must also be accessible to these children. So I chose this psalm to name the problem.
>
> "See I will bring a scroll recounting what befell me": This verse names one of the basic tools I've been using. I get them to recount their stories, and I tell them that I value the stories by listening to them and by recording their complaints. But it is so little.
>
> "I trust in the faithfulness of God forever and ever": I both do and don't. Part of me feels it is selfish or unfeeling of me to trust in God's faithfulness in the face of such real suffering.

Is trust selfish? Is it wrong to hope? Hope is not a wish for a specific outcome but a fundamental stance of openness before the
world. Joan struggled with this idea: hope and trust felt to her like
genuine goods, like gifts in bad times, but she didn't want to offer
some easy pacifier to quiet her moral outrage. She concluded with:

> "But God is the stay of my mind, my portion forever": Do you
> remember the months we spent with our differing interpreta-
> tions of Psalm 73? I still have my old copy of the Book of
> Psalms, and I underlined the passages you thought were crucial
> in blue and the ones I thought were the key to the psalm in red.
> Here was this line we looked at before, but now I see it in a
> totally different way.
>
> I chose: "Whom else have I in heaven? / And having You, I want
> no one on earth." I had thought it was about absolute isolation,
> but you kept me focused on the fullness of life lived with God.
> Then I chose the line, "My body and mind fail," but you countered
> with "But God is the stay of my mind, my portion forever."
>
> It's taken me six years, but I'm beginning to see that this is
> the crucial line in the psalm. As you rightly guessed, I'm still
> interested in playing with both the psalms and creativity.
> Spirituality and creativity are both more ordinary and more
> wondrous than people generally admit. I've come to see that the
> spiritual life is not something you focus *on* but something you
> focus *with*. I wish I could say that better. The focus should not
> be *on* the self, it should *use* the self. I believe that creativity is a
> profound form of worship and that both spirituality and cre-
> ativity aim for us to be fully alive.
>
> I don't want the Book of Psalms to be my security blanket or
> the harbor where I take refuge. I want it to be the trumpet blare
> that sends us off to challenge an unjust world, or, to return to
> my harbor image, it must be the harbor from which we set sail.
> That was a great metaphor I read in Kazantzakis's *Report to
> Greco*: harbors are both shelters and embarkation points for
> great adventures.

Joan's remarks left me a little breathless, with all she had done in the time since our last meeting. And still she soldiered on:

> When I try to focus on what concerns me most fully, I realize it is *not* creativity. Creativity sounds too much like what authors are concerned with when people have writer's block. My concern is world making—creating or discovering a way to make sense of my role in the system as a whole. I'm concerned with value making: ethics, aesthetics, the creation of human institutions. What I thought about when I first worked with you was a book I wanted to write. You even gave me a title: "Psalms: A Journey of Creativity," and I read a bunch of books about art and artists. It is clearly an area that engaged me and continues to engage me. But my deepest concern is with creating my own self, my world, my sense of my life. And that really is consistent with what I want to do in social work, even if it is not the most orthodox approach.

Joan was fighting a war against degradation and death by creating. Daily, she faced the horrors of child abuse and the difficulties of finding placements for abandoned kids. She had to return to her own creativity—the art, the journey through the psalms—and somehow offer her vision of world making to her clients.

Over time, Joan explained why her spiritual work was so deeply connected with her work in the BCW. She told me about some of the cases and tried to express what she was hoping her clients would recognize:

> I must show them that the world as they have conceived it does not account for all of reality, and then I must help them remake it around a new center. The differences between what the mystics call the dark night of the soul and hell, or torture, are that after the dark night comes a new creation.

Part of Joan's frustration in her work came because it's really hard to pass on a new vision of reality. She was right that a new under-

standing of the world and their place in it would open up possibili-
ties for her clients that could be genuinely liberating, but all she could
do was invite and evoke.

For many months all I could do was encourage and support. Not
even someone as alive and dedicated as Joan could turn around the
BCW single-handedly. I was, therefore, amazed when Joan came to
see me, eyes sparkling, and announced, "I'm in love."

I looked at her, and she laughed:

> I mean, the world is so wonderful and I'm so excited, it feels as
> though I'm in love. I have a nine-year-old client, Elio. He has a
> really sad background. When I read his case, I didn't know
> whether to cry or to get a gun and kill all those uncaring people
> who had moved him around so much. When I met him at his
> current foster home, I was struck by how small and very skinny
> he was. He sat sullenly at the other side of the table and didn't
> respond to a single question I asked. I couldn't even imagine
> him smiling. Then something wonderful happened. After the
> third time I saw you, I went back to carrying one of these large
> war surplus bags. I loaded it up with charcoal, blank book, pen-
> cils, sharpener, and the Book of Psalms. At my next meeting with
> Elio, I reached into my bag, handed him some charcoal and a
> blank piece of paper, and asked him to draw his home. He still
> hadn't said anything, but he began to draw. Within less than two
> minutes, he seemed to forget I was there and was totally into his
> drawing. After a while, I asked him to tell me something about
> his drawing, and without looking up, he started talking. So, you
> could say this was a good way beyond an impasse, but that
> wasn't all.

She paused and smiled, as if she were about to reveal a great
secret, and then added:

> His drawing was good! Powerful. I gave him a fresh piece of
> paper, asked him about his brother, and he was off and drawing

again. In the process, I learned that he missed his brother very much and that his brother had one blind eye. His drawing had an immediacy and balance that you don't usually see in little kids' drawings.

Well, the next time I went to see Elio, he sat right down and pointed to my bag. I was prepared, and out came not only paper and charcoal, but even some pastels, if he wanted to work in color. Our meetings continued. When I looked over his records, I realized that the following week would be his ninth birthday. I checked with his foster mother and arranged my schedule so that he would be the last client I saw that day. He went over to the table as usual, but I said we would not be meeting there, that we were going out. He came along and even held my hand without protest as we crossed a busy intersection. We had to take two buses, and then we climbed the stairs to the Metropolitan Museum of Art. I showed him some of the highlights of the permanent collection and explained to him that some people like to draw in the museum. I then took out a small blank book, a box of charcoal, and a kneaded eraser, gave him the supplies, and told him to look around in the gallery I had chosen. I then told the guard that this was my special friend and he was not to be disturbed—I would be in the next gallery. I looked in after fifteen minutes—it was hard not to look sooner—and Elio was sitting on the floor with his tongue sticking out between his teeth, copying Van Gogh's drawing of a pair of workingman's shoes. I left and returned as he was finishing his drawing. I told him to keep the charcoal and sketchbook as my birthday present to him.

Joan held up her hand to show me she was not finished with the story.

That was three weeks ago. When I saw Elio again this morning, he handed me a big envelope with my name on it. In it were five more of his drawings—copies of paintings that are in a different gallery at the Met. Now do you see why I'm in love?

She then reached into her war surplus bag, pulled out the psalms, and read from Psalm 40:3–4: "He lifted me out of the miry pit, / the slimy clay, / and set my feet on a rock, / steadied my legs. / God put a new song into my mouth." Then she said, "I think the next time I see Elio I'm going to ask him to draw his hand. Maybe then he, too, can be even more aware of a relationship that can give him freedom and joy."

15

MARION
The Gift of Creativity That Saves a Marriage

I first met Marion when she was forty-six years old. She had dark eyes
and dark hair pulled back into a bun. Her skin had the warm tone of
the Mediterranean, and her speech was accented with both French,
her native language, and Arabic, which she learned in childhood. She
lived in Waltham, Massachusetts, a suburb west of Boston. She came
to see me to talk about problems in her marriage.

During the first three years of her twenty-two-year marriage to
Albert, she taught foreign languages. After that, she gave full attention to raising her three children, the oldest of whom, her daughter
Audrey, was poised to enter college. Her middle daughter, Betsy, was
a junior in high school and her youngest, Caroline (Marion claimed
that naming her children alphabetically was purely accidental), was
in sixth grade.

When Caroline entered school, Marion had wanted to return to
teaching, but Albert said he had grown accustomed to her being
home, always available to meet his needs. He was in the leather
import business, partnered with a man who had immigrated with
them when they fled Morocco shortly after they married. Not long
after her arrival in the United States, Marion got word that Jon, her
beloved younger brother, had died in an auto accident back home,

leaving her feeling more cut off from the world she had always known. Albert worked long hours, and when he returned home, he would retire to his "study," the one free room in their sprawling but crowded house. She could expect no help with raising the children, not their science projects nor their French homework (although Albert, like Marion, spoke French fluently) nor their regular mini-crises. She drove the car pools, kept the car gassed and serviced, cleaned up after three children and one husband, did the shopping and the laundry, and saw to the myriad details of keeping a house and a family in working order.

After nineteen years of all this, Marion had fallen into a deep depression. It wasn't only their finances—she was not sure whether their money was really tight or her husband stingy. He always seemed to have enough money for the books and expensive stereo equipment he wanted. Nor was it the children all being adolescents at once—surely a trial for anyone. But she no longer knew why she should want to get up in the mornings. Marion described her experience very tentatively. She kept watching to see if I would disapprove or disbelieve. I listened with unfeigned interest as she described a recent incident:

> Last Friday night, I went to Shabbat services, which Albert hasn't attended for years, and I stayed after everyone had left. I waited in a corner, and after the crowd left and the lights were turned down, I walked to my bench near the back of the synagogue and moved into my seat. I began to pray and found the seated position was inadequate. So I got down on my knees—

At this point Marion looked to see if I would disapprove, because getting on your knees is forbidden to strictly observant Jews. I had no feelings about it either way, so I had no trouble keeping a neutral look.

> —and I just kept repeating, "God, tell me what to do." I have no idea how long I knelt there, but suddenly I saw an image

forming behind my closed eyelids. A hand was writing on a blackboard. I watched as the words formed "you should write." Then the image disappeared. There I was in the synagogue, praying for a way to deal with the children, with my husband's demands, with our supposedly small budget, and with my frustration, and I was shocked through and through. Here I was, asking for a bowl of soup, and I was given a bowl of flowers!

I left the synagogue and went home, but all week long, the image of the writing hand and the words "you should write" kept coming back to me. Finally, I decided that if it really was a vision, I shouldn't dismiss it but try to understand it. I waited until the house was empty, sat down in the second most comfortable easy chair in the house (the best one is in Albert's den), and tried to recall when in my life I'd been happiest. I was quickly transported back to my school days. I lived at home with my parents when I went to upper school, but after lycée, I could move away to a new city and find a job because I was educated. I had a wonderful circle of friends, and we spent hours sharing ideas and dreaming dreams. I never felt more alive, and I never got to know a group of people as exciting as they were. But you're going to think that's crazy! Hadn't I been thrilled when my children were born? Hadn't—

I told her to stop being defensive and just follow her thoughts. She realized that it had been many years since she had allowed herself to think about those university days.

I had friends, we had endless discussions about theater and politics, and my mind was opening up in many exciting ways. I used to write during that time. Everybody I knew was an artist, an actor, a poet, and each one was also a philosopher, an intellectual, a critic—you get the idea. It was hard to leave my friends behind when we moved to the States, but it was clear that the political situation was getting worse and worse for Jews. The hardest part was leaving my brother, Jon. I couldn't know when we emigrated that I would never see him again. He was at our wedding and saw us off when we left Morocco, but shortly after we arrived here, he died in a car accident.

For a moment she was lost in the sad memory, then she shook her head and continued with her remarks:

Well, with all the many moves during our first years here—from state to state, from apartment to house, then back to apartment and back to house—nothing remained of my old notebooks. But I do remember, not what I wrote, but how it felt to be writing. There is the sweet secret of an idea germinating within, then growing and taking shape.

When I next saw Marion, she told me she had taken a thin notebook with a few old magazine recipes pasted in it. She pulled out the recipes "with malicious pleasure," she said, and tentatively wrote a date in it. She recorded the vision and some of her feelings about it, then carefully hid the notebook under the undergarments in her dresser.

At her next free moment, she composed a few tentative poems, then suddenly felt that what she really had to write was a play. By now she had secured a package containing four smallish pads of Post-its, a significant purchase for her because it was the first thing she could remember buying in the United States that wasn't something for the family or clothing and toiletries for herself. One blank pad always lived in her pocketbook, so she could write down ideas, bits of conversation, images that struck her, and memories that surfaced after being lost for years. When she got home, she would paste all the used Post-its for that day into her notebook. Many of the jottings eventually found their way into the play she had begun writing. Finally, she bought a new notebook, one of those with a mottled black-and-white hard cover and a mock label in the middle containing the word "Compositions" in large type and a few lines for name and address. Into this "composition" book she carefully copied material that felt polished.

She began visiting her branch library regularly and took out plays by some of her favorite authors, such as Molière, Racine, Schnitzler, and Shaw, and the occasional book on writing. If her branch lacked a title she was seeking, she asked to have it ordered on interlibrary loan. Here this put-upon woman had suddenly woken up to the realization that she could have a life of her own, even if it was only for an hour or two per day and even though she had to keep her activity secret.

At a session soon after she disclosed her clandestine writing, Marion reported to me in the old, deadened voice she had used before her vision:

> Audrey had a serious fight with her father last week about cur-
> few. Albert has very little to do with raising the kids, but he's
> still the chief disciplinarian in the house and makes all the rules.
> Audrey just graduated from high school, as you know, and she
> wants some of the privileges and freedoms that someone about
> to go off to college deserves. After all, she is not from the old
> country; she doesn't have to follow all the old ways. I felt awful
> watching the fight between the two, and then I saw Audrey
> glance toward me, but she quickly turned away with a look of
> disgust. How have I let my life get like this? I had strength,
> courage, and fervor in my student days. I want Audrey to have
> the same freedom I had, and yet, at the crucial moment, I was
> silent. Long after Audrey went to her room and Albert had gone
> to sleep, I was still exploring the pain I felt from their fight. I
> kept remembering my student days, when I had felt so alive.
> Some of that excitement began to return as I started to write.
> Writing for me has been an amazing gift—but it has come with
> pain. It feels like the return of sensation when Novocain wears
> off—it is a relief to be able to feel your mouth and jaw again,
> but along with that feeling comes the pain where the tooth has
> been extracted.

So now Marion felt the dimensions of her life much more clearly than she ever had, and she also felt the pain at allowing so much freedom to be taken from her. Her oldest daughter had obviously decided that she could not look to her mother for a model, or even for support. Was there any way she could recover her daughter's respect?

A writer is a writer because of what she perceives, not because of what she writes—so, even on days when she didn't write at all, Marion's way of interacting with people, places, and events over the following year changed radically. She never explicitly addressed Audrey's struggle with her father. Instead, she decided that the dispute was only one incident in an entire life. Children are such absolutists: either you are their saint and hero or you are banished into outer darkness. From Marion's perspective, it was essential to go beyond a single incident to a life, a life with all of its blessing and curses. As Marion put it:

> What is a life? Not just lilacs and dew on the grass in the early morning, but the cat litter box to be cleaned out and the smoke from the backup of the exhaust fan over the stove when it gets blocked up. I want the whole thing! When I found myself writing a poem about the exhaust fan, I had to burst out laughing.

Her sense of humor was waking up and stretching.

One day she recalled an old flip-flop book the children had when they were much younger. The book was sliced across the middle and you moved different heads onto different bodies. So Mr. Pig's head landed on a horse or a schoolteacher; and Mr. Fish's tail was attached to the family dog or the letter carrier. What a wonderful idea! What if she could attach the chimp's tail to her husband? Would he be more playful? Would he be drawn to swinging on trees?

Whatever Audrey had previously thought about her mother, she was quick to notice the change—Marion was far more alive. When Marion recognized that her daughter was actually seeing her, she decided to share part of her secret. With her daughter due to go off to college at the end of the summer, Marion knew they needed to talk. She explained to her husband that she had to have some mother-daughter time with Audrey, so after seeing that the other children were busy, she and Audrey went for a long drive into the country. Slowly and deliberately she told her daughter what her own education had meant to her. She wanted to convey to Audrey that it was important for her to discover what she really loved and to find joy in her studies. Marion was not one to lecture; instead, she confided that she was writing and showed Audrey three poems she had written and a scene from the play.

A month later, with Audrey safely ensconced at Mount Holyoke College, Marion told me:

> Audrey seemed grateful for our time together and for a chance to talk as one adult to another. She swore to me she'd keep my secret, and guess what! She just sent me a birthday package. I was home alone when the package was delivered and opened it in privacy. It was a lap desk—a narrow box with a slanted wooden surface and a firm pillow below. The top lifts up, and I found she had put in a box of twelve number 3 pencils (how does she know that's what I use?), an eraser, and a funny metal pencil sharpener in the shape of an upright piano. And there was the most elegant blank book I have ever seen. It has a dark leather cover and a gold ribbon place mark. I can't tell you what it means to me.

Marion's audience was always very small. She shared her plays— the initial play grew into a trilogy—with a friend she had made when both their children were young (the husbands never met); with Audrey; with Susan, a woman who encouraged her and even offered to input her writing into a computer (Marion had no computer, so she handwrote all her work); and with me. Her husband allowed her to go on a retreat with me. It never occurred to him that the retreat was anything other than some gathering of people who prayed. In fact, it was an undirected retreat that was a chance for both of us to spend time alone together on the rocks of Gloucester, Massachusetts, and to share our writing, our process, and all that grew out of it.

Marion had been religious, if not observant, faithful in prayer, but there was a real gap between behaving correctly according to her Jewish traditions and addressing the large questions in her life. It was desperation that led her to pray that fateful day, and her vision of the hand telling her "you should write" changed all her views about religion. From that day on, she said, she understood that she was important, loved, and obliged to recognize and use her gifts. She needed only one miracle, because she was so jolted into awakening that each day saw her increasingly open to the world around her. Writing was both a gift and a miracle.

So far, only the three small poems that Marion showed Audrey had been published, under a pen name, in the local newspaper. The gift of Marion's writing was the gift of her seeing, hearing, tasting— experiencing. It was also the gift of her reading other poets and writers. Her liberation was the greatest gift she could have given Audrey on her way to college. Instead of worrying about her mother, Audrey was free to explore her own interests and dreams. Marion's writing was not just a matter of producing poems; it represented a transformation of her being in the world that included a new appreciation of nature, music, literature, and many other facets of life—and, even more important, a new way of relating to her daughter. Religion was not simply one area of Marion's life, writing another, nature another, relationships another—it was, as it is in all of us, the transformation of her *perception* in all these areas. Marion had discovered the confluence of her religious and creative life.

In addition to actual writing, Marion recorded occasional comments about writers and writing. One of the first of these barked out: "The way to write is by writing—daily—forever." As this remark suggests, the call to write was not without difficulties. She was soon setting goals for herself—number of pages written, number of scenes completed. It was then that she found doubt creeping in, and she wrote about her first experience, albeit brief, of writer's block. Increasingly, though, her remarks doubted her own writing ability. Fortunately, these discouraging notations turned out to be very useful. Together we were able to discover patterns in her negative feelings.

Her first doubt questioned the value of what she was doing: "I have to get clear on what is different in what I'm trying to do." Working through that issue, she recognized that she couldn't keep her own first commandment, writing daily forever, if she didn't find a commitment deeper than momentary "highs":

> I need a creativity for the long term. Beyond overcoming my doubting inner voice, I must accept my responsibility for creating meaningful worlds. I have to create as a response to the life, energy, beauty, and inspiration I have been given. I want to smile back to the universe, give birth to my own ideas, be fruitful and multiply, and make apparent what other people overlook.

Marion showed me the questions she had written in her notebook and her answers:

> 1. *What do I want to put into the world?* That remains a burning issue for me. I want to contribute. I want to write a novel, or a play, or an epic poem—I still can't figure out which—that convinces people that their lives are important, that they have something unique to contribute, and that discovering what it is would take them on a magnificent adventure. I want them to find a world of challenges and depth that is free of all the trivialities that the TV wants us to focus on. They should see how wonderful life really is—an adventure that is much greater than the distractions of fashion and consumerism and little matters and small tasks. I want to call them to serve the good, the true, and the beautiful; then they would find true freedom.
>
> 2. *Out of what is my world made?* I'm trying to figure out what constitutes my world. I have chosen the world of language, of literary form, of assonance and simile and metaphor. But beyond these elements lies the question of what values and meaning are expressed through them.
>
> 3. *How can I bring my worldview to others?* How can I become a bridge that allows someone else to see my world? How do I

begin to share my perceptions and insights? I know I can't simply say it; I have to show it or evoke it.

4. *How can I become aware of my own mistakes?* I now consider my rough drafts and earlier versions to be a different way of seeing the world. I'm less eager to evaluate than to learn from what I'm doing. I guess this connects with another thought I had:

5. *When is a poem or a play finished?* Not when it comes out of the printer, of that I'm sure. When I first saw my writing in printed form, thanks to Susan's inputting and printing it for me, it looked like a cake that was too beautiful to cut. I don't mean the content; I mean the lovely printing. I couldn't bear to write on it. Then Susan showed me how easy it is to make a change on the computer and print out a new version. After that I could see the printed text as something new with which I could interact.

Several years after Marion had started seeing me, she summarized what she had arrived at:

> Writing is not about producing books. If it were, Ecclesiastes would be right: "The making of many books is without limit, and much study is a wearying of the flesh." Maybe the making of books is without limit, but my writing can be a place where I can come to God and God can come to me. It can be like a rendezvous. I write in order to think, and I share my thoughts. I need to think through if and how the Jewish symbol system can express my experience of being alive. I start with my life, and I cannot reflect on my life without language. Sometimes I dream of posthumous publication, because I want my writing to be a place where I can offer any insights I might have, but with my ego totally removed.
>
> I guess my major conclusion is that writing has been and still is a gift. Sometimes, it is the place where I encounter God, but even when I don't, it is an occasion of discovery.

I asked Marion what she had learned from all of this. She didn't hesitate: "I learned that God cares about me—even about the smallest details of my life." Then, after a moment, she added, "Whoever said it was right—we find God wherever we let God in."

I was delighted with her upbeat conclusion but couldn't help remembering that her brother had died in a car accident shortly after she was married. And as if she could read my mind, she said:

> I still miss Jon—I guess I always will. He believed in me. He was my little brother and my biggest supporter. But I never thought he was distant from God. Look, I still have tensions with Albert, and now Betsy is doing the college search. The problems don't go away, but I now have a place to stand. I stand, with certainty, in my relationship to God. God has given me the gift to write, which is the gift to see and be awake and aware. God has given me my freedom so that I can release my daughters and let them fly. Amidst the pain and tension—God has given me joy.

16

MAUREEN

Remaining a Jew-by-Choice after the Children Are Grown

Maureen had been a Conservative Jew for more than twenty years and had raised a daughter and a son in her faith, but as a "Jew-by-choice," she did not allow herself to raise questions. Still, she somehow believed that members of her congregation could never accept her as fully Jewish, although she wondered if she was not simply projecting her own feelings onto them. She wanted to know whether any rite could ever make her feel more authentically Jewish—her children's b'nei mitzvah and her own adult bat mitzvah didn't quite do it. "Should I start using 'Miriam,' the Hebrew name they gave me?" she asked. "If we aren't born into a religion, can it ever really feel like ours? Is it un-Jewish to like the smell of pine at Christmas? Is it wrong to miss things I had loved about Christianity, such as grace and the beatitudes?"

Maureen's fiery red-orange hair literally glowed in the sunshine. Combined with her pale skin, freckles, and the green tops she usually wore, her looks practically screamed "Irish." But her pronunciation of *chutzpah, baruch HaShem,* and other Yiddish and Hebrew expressions, not to mention her regular use of them, made it clear to which community she belonged. Her story, moreover, indicated that she had converted out of an inner desire, not merely to please her husband or in-laws:

To begin at the beginning, I'm a born and bred New Yorker. I'm a graduate of Julia Richman High School, and I made it into Oberlin College. I went there because I thought it would be good to get out of town and because the school was a hotbed of liberalism. In my junior year—that would be twenty-one years ago—I met Ron, who became my boyfriend. Ron was Jewish, and he took me as his date to a mixer (how apt the word!) and a Friday night dinner at Hillel. We also attended a Chanukah party there and joined in some other activities. As our relationship deepened, I began asking him about his faith, but soon, instead of answering, he suggested we take a course together. It seemed like too serious a step, not something you would ask a casual date to do. I stopped talking about Judaism with him, but on my own I attended a Shabbat service at a nearby synagogue without him; I wanted to find out if I would get the same warm feelings when the man I loved wasn't there.

After *Aleinu* and a few announcements, I asked the rabbi if I could make an appointment to see him. That was scary, but he was very down-to-earth, so when I came to his office at the synagogue, he made me feel comfortable right away. I explained that I wanted to learn more about Judaism, but I didn't want to confuse that with my growing relationship with Ron. The rabbi said I was most welcome to continue coming to services, and he also lent me a book. Then he told me he would be teaching a course at the synagogue, which would start again in a month.

She paused, rearranged herself in her seat, and then continued:

What's so funny about all this, is that by the time the Introduction to Judaism course started, Ron and I were no longer seeing one another. Well, no, that's not the funny thing— the funny thing is that I took the course anyway. No matter that I had been giving the "right" answer to the rabbi—I wasn't studying Judaism because of a boyfriend, but because the religion itself drew me—it was also the true answer. It was six months later that I met my husband, Saul. And, not surprisingly, he was Jewish, and I was well on the way to becoming Jewish.

Maureen's early years as a Jew were filled with moments of intense prayer. She loved lighting Friday night candles and making the special foods appropriate for each holiday: hamantaschen for Purim, potato latkes for Chanukah, cheesecake for Shavuot, and the like. She brought much of her own warmth to her celebration of the festivals so that her daughter, Sally, and her son, Jack, felt they had grown up in a very Jewish home. She couldn't understand how some Jews she knew actually put up a Christmas tree and exchanged Christmas presents. The excuse that it was no longer a religious holiday struck her as disingenuous or, at best, wishful thinking.

Now, with the children away from home, she admitted that it had been many years since she had felt moved by the services. Her beliefs hadn't changed, but her feelings had. It all, somehow, seemed routine. It made sense to put up a sukkah when the children were home—now it was just a chore. She didn't even feel like lighting candles on Chanukah. She missed the children, and she felt it especially when she thought of the many years they lit candles together and then sang "Maoz Tzur" and all their favorite Chanukah songs. Now, with just her and Saul at home, the ritual seemed a bit silly, and the singing felt hollow. She also cut way back on cooking and baked only rarely. Passover, though, remained wonderful because the children managed to come home for the seder from wherever they were.

"Am I falling out of love?" she asked. "Am I having a midlife crisis of my faith?"

Maureen was shaken when she realized that her daughter was the same age she was when she became a Jew-by-choice. Had Maureen prepared Sally adequately for encountering diversity and confusion at college? And how much does she, herself, really believe? I asked her if she could say what the world looks like to a believing Jew. Did she remember what it had looked like after she had decided to convert but before she had met her husband?

I don't remember my father ever going to church. He must have, at least for my first communion, but I can't remember it. After my grandmother—my mother's mother—died, my mother didn't go to church anymore, either. So it was no big deal for them when I began dating Ron. But when Ron and I broke up and I still continued to study Judaism, that surprised them. As my mother put it, "I thought this Judaism thing was a prerequisite for Ron." That remark, however slight, was the only negative comment I heard at home about the prospect of my converting. My mom wanted to know if I would still eat in their house and would my kids come over for Christmas. I said of course, and we joke that we go religiously every year.

We've never had a problem with nieces and nephews, either. It's all been surprisingly easy, in part because we all celebrate everything. For Passover, Saul's family has us over the first night, and we have my family over the second night— thank goodness there are two seders! The kids are clear that they are Jewish, and our celebrations at home and in Hebrew school were sufficiently joyous that Christmas never tempted them. I sometimes think the ease with which we glided through this potential minefield called religion is due to my in-laws' unreconstructed Marxism and my parents' obvious disdain for other Catholics in general and church services in particular.

Maureen explained that part of what drew her to Saul was a certain seriousness he had—call it a focus. He seemed to know who he was and what he was about.

"Did that turn out to be true?" I asked.

"To a remarkable degree, yes."

"Why do you think that is?"

"Judaism," she replied, "gives him a lens through which to view everything, whether it's politics or economics, ethics or ecology, even child rearing. You name it, and he has a Jewish take on it."

I asked her what she thought of this lens.

It obviously works very well—I mean, Saul is one of the most caring and ethical people I know. For him, the children's upbringing took precedence over everything, even his advancement at work. We share the same values; in fact, when he was dating me, he used to tell me I had a Jewish *n'shamah*, a Jewish soul—he meant I'd gotten to the same political and ethical positions without having the Jewish background.

"Do you and he still share the same values?"

"Yes," she said.

"So tell me what's wrong."

"I don't feel the same way anymore about being Jewish."

I asked her if she meant that the thrill was gone.

"Something like that—it's hard to really care about the holidays when there are no children at home."

She laughed when I replied, "That's why God invented grandchildren."

OK—but it's more serious than that. I've been active in our synagogue since the kids were in preschool, but I've always been—I don't know—compliant. It was enough that I stood out with my red hair and small nose and my very un-Jewish name—I didn't feel I had the right to get into debates about the rabbi's sermons or synagogue policy.

"In other words, even though you were active in the synagogue for twenty years, you felt like a visitor in someone else's home."

"Exactly," she said.

"You never thought of yourself as a Jew, but as a Jew-by-choice."

"Right."

"Have the people in the synagogue made you feel that way?" I asked.

"No. They long ago accepted that I'm a Jew."

"So what's new? What changed?"

She replied:

I guess this sounds silly: I want to feel authentic. I don't want to simply "pass" as a Jew—knowing all the little rules about kashrut and Passover. Saul says I actually know more rules than he does. OK, I've studied a lot and taken all the adult ed courses, but I still feel as if I'm playing a role—being tested or something.

"Leaving aside the synagogue thing a moment, and even the family celebrations, what do you believe when you're all alone by yourself?" I asked.

"What do I believe about what?"

"When you were still in college, Saul told you you had a Jewish *n'shamah*. What do you believe about who we are and what life is about? How do you relate to God?"

That's one of my concerns: the Jews I know never really talk about God. Since earliest childhood—my pre-Jewish childhood, that is—I have always prayed, and not from a book. I always had an ongoing conversation with God. After converting, though, I wondered if I could continue praying as I had.

I asked her to tell me a little more about this ongoing conversation with God. She said:

I dropped out of church in what would have been the sixth grade of Sunday school, so I don't exactly have an adult perspective. But what I had learned about prayer by then was that we often have this little figure in our mind sorting things out, noticing what we're doing, reacting to what is good and what is not so good, and guiding us accordingly. I was told that the little figure is really God, and I should stop periodically during the day and deliberately notice, and even talk to, this inner figure. It was funny—when we played hide-and-go-seek and I hid in the smallest place I could crawl into, the figure, really God, was with me. Sometimes I wished God would look away after I had done something particularly nasty, but I also felt I was not alone and I could pick up the conversation wherever I was.

"Did you discuss this with the rabbi?"
"No," she said,

> I didn't feel comfortable raising it. When the kids were growing up, I taught them to say the *Sh'ma*, but it felt impersonal —it was the Jewish prayer, but it wasn't their personal prayer. What they brought home from Hebrew school never touched on their relationship to God. I learned, through them, more Jewish history, Bible stories, holiday lore than I ever wanted to know. Later, they got into other questions, but they never discussed the things *I* was thinking about, like the way God lives inside every one of us. Instead, they talked about whether Jews have a unique mission and why there are so many Jewish musicians, comedians, and writers, but not painters.

Had she ever discussed any of this with Saul?
"No, he thinks the sum of Judaism is 'be a mensch,' and I can't argue with that. But that's not all—in fact, you can't even be that without God."
"Did your children ever ask you about God?"

> No, I hoped they would, but they were more like Saul about religion—that's one reason I began to feel that maybe the conversion hadn't taken. Maybe on some deep level I still have a Christian worldview.

"It seems to me that you are describing two distinct problems that are related but are really separate. One has to do with whether or not you are really Jewish; the other has to do with some change in your relationship with God."
"Exactly."

I told Maureen that I thought the second question should come first, because I didn't think there was any question about her being Jewish—and that she had finally taken on an essential Jewish characteristic, the willingness to argue. I also said that I thought her relationship to Judaism was only a means to the primary end, her relationship with God. Judaism is her way to God, I said, but God is not the private property of Judaism. "You were a beloved child of God long before you converted—and, undoubtedly, you already had a relationship with God."

"Yes—I thought I did, but I didn't know what to do with all my earlier experiences and feelings once I'd converted."

"So you forgot them?"

"Something like that."

I became fascinated with a little dance step Maureen was doing even as she sat in her seat. Her left foot would advance, pull back, her right foot would cross over to the left, and all the while she sat absolutely erect and unmoving above the waist. "And now?" I asked.

"I can't play games anymore. I really want to get back to a regular, authentic relationship to God."

How did she want to begin?

"It was so easy and natural when I was a little girl, but now I feel, well, embarrassed."

I told her that this was a process of discovering what felt natural for her. "You can begin very simply—just saying thank-you for a beautiful day—or anything else you want to express gratitude for. When you feel ready you can do more."

"I don't want you to think I haven't prayed all these years—" she said,

> I have, but it hasn't been regular, it hasn't been part of an ongoing relationship. I always said the prayers in synagogue, and occasionally they felt like my words, but only very occasionally. And, of course, I prayed when my father had a heart attack—a kind of desperation prayer. But the easy, ongoing conversational prayer I had in my childhood got lost when I converted. I'm really not sure how to start it again.

When I asked her if she kept a journal, she said yes. "Suppose, then, the next time you write in it, you make it a letter to God. You could say all the things you haven't been able to express for a long time."

She thought this over, then nodded and said she would try.

When I next saw Maureen, she told me the journal idea had really "broken the ice"; in fact, so much had happened, she was glad the children were not still at home, because keeping the journal took so much of her time and attention. "When I began," she said, "I was certain I was looking for God. Now I'm not so sure."

"What do you mean?"

"Well, when I started to pray again, it seemed to me that God had been looking for me and it was me who finally answered the phone."

She stopped, caught her breath, and continued, more slowly:

> I don't know why I ever thought talking to God was not a Jewish thing. I'm always reading the psalms, I saw *Fiddler on the Roof* three times, twice in a school production that my kids played in. Tevye is constantly talking to God—I mean, you were right. The real issue is not whether I am an authentic Jew; it is my relationship to God. And, I guess I made another discovery.

She continued, speaking even more slowly and somewhat hesitantly, as she seemed to find saying the words very difficult:

> All these years that I've stopped praying to God, I blamed my conversion. But that wasn't it. I'm the one who stopped—no one made me. I stopped because I was frightened. When you're in college and you want to have kids or you're busy making a home and raising a family, it's scary to think that your life is about a relationship to God. I just wanted an ordinary life.

Her eyes began to tear up, so I motioned to the box of tissues that I always keep on my desk next to the guest chair. She pulled one out and blew her nose. "And now?" I asked.

The kids are launched, Saul is an autonomous adult, so I'm not really taking anyone else along for the ride who doesn't want to come. I've been a coward for too long, and I'm *still* frightened. But now I'm determined to live the life I was meant to live, so I'm ready to pray again.

"Slow down," I said, "you're racing ahead. I want to know how you went from years of silence to this sudden sense that your life has taken a whole new direction."

I knew when I left your office that I had something very exciting to do. Somehow I got through dinner, and then I went into Jack's old room, which I had turned into my study. I took out my journal—I thought maybe I should buy a new one for the occasion, but then I realized I was just procrastinating. It was hard, let me tell you.

I set out to pray, and as I began to think, I became aware of why I hadn't prayed all these years. Do you know what would be at stake if people knew God was real? Not just that the idea of God makes sense, but that God is real and waiting? Let me make a comparison: We know that death is real, so we exercise realistic precautions (we get annual checkups and we don't jump out of the window), but for the most part, we hide the reality of death from ourselves so we can get on with our ordinary lives. I was fascinated to learn that monks in the Middle Ages used to keep a skull in their cell as a *memento mori*, a reminder of death. But these were religious contemplatives, not people who raised children, held down ordinary jobs, and built families.

In the same way that death is real, so is God. And I'm sure there are contemplatives and hermits who live with that reality daily before them, but I can't imagine knowing that and still packing school lunches or getting the children to do their homework, or, well, all the ordinary things we do.

She settled back in her chair and ran the back of her hand across her forehead in a motion that expressed a mocking "whew." I waited a moment and then said, "You've made a good case for not fully taking in the reality of God, so why are you now returning to prayer?"

She replied:

I guess it was easy to understand—although I think none of this was fully conscious—how powerful and scary God's presence can be, but it took much longer to figure out how deadening God's absence is. Go back to my analogy of death: We know how fear of death can be paralyzing. But we shouldn't simply be fearless; we have to find some sort of balance or proportion. I remember how difficult it was to teach our children some sort of balance between their natural curiosity and the caution they needed just to survive.

In my childhood, I wasn't at all cautious about being close to God. I was never a good Catholic—I didn't like Sunday school, I didn't like church, but I did like to pray. At the time, I didn't know enough to realize that prayer is scary business, and it all felt natural. I think I got self-conscious about it during my senior year in high school. I was seeing something my friends weren't seeing—I don't know how else to express it. They teased me, good-naturedly, that I was too serious or intense, but I didn't know how to forget everything and party the way they did. They not only forgot God, which I really couldn't do, they also forgot death. A few of my classmates were hurt in car accidents, and one boy actually got his neck broken in a diving accident at a beach party to celebrate the end of school. I sensed the danger of forgetting God, but I also hated the social isolation of remembering. God, that sounds so awful! Did I really turn away from God in order to be popular?

College was a better time. Lots of people were serious about ideas, about discovering what they wanted to study, about politics. I met Saul at a teach-in to discuss migrant workers. I was attracted both by his good looks and by the thoughtful remarks he made at that meeting. Is it possible—I don't want to think it's possible—that I went the whole conversion route just to avoid praying?

"You are assuming that becoming Jewish was a detour and that these past twenty-odd years were a mistake," I interjected.

"No, no," she replied, "I wouldn't say that. It's just that once I converted, I could really spend years and years being involved in religion but at the same time avoiding God."

"Avoiding God, or avoiding one specific image of God? I think it's no accident that the analogy you used for remembering God was the monks remembering death. The God-image you probably had before college was of a life-denying 'other.' Now you've had all these years of a life rich in love of husband and children and suffused with the presence of God."

"But Jews don't talk about God. They're concerned with history, tradition, and custom, but not about relationship," she said.

"Wait, you're the one who told me about the psalms and Tevye. Anyhow, talking *about* God isn't what you're after, it's talking *to* God. I suggested that your earlier view of God was one of radical otherness—an image that distances God from our ordinary world. Your past twenty years have centered on God found in and through your relationships with your family. Let me draw you images of three different worldviews:

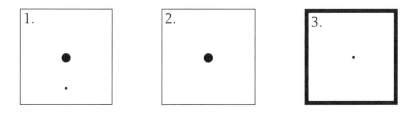

"Number 1 represents the traditional image of God and world. God is "up there" and we are down here, and there is that unbridgeable space in between. God comes to the world through creation, revelation, and miracle, but God is transcendent and remote. Mystics

spoke of being happy to have 'a ladder in their own house,' expressing their desire for some way to cross that divide.

"Number 2 represents a pantheist image of God, showing that
everything is God, or, God is in everything. But if you are a secular
humanist, the dot represents the world, which is all there is.

"Number 3 represents an image in which God is the *place* of the
world (*HaMakom*). There is no place without God, but the world is
not God's place. We are part of God, but God is not reduced to what
we can experience or know. We can find evidence of God within, and
we can find evidence of God if we look at the distant stars. To put it
another way: we can learn a lot about the sun by seeing how it illu-
minates everything we look at—trees, animals, buildings. We love the
light and the energy that makes life and growth possible, but we cannot look at the sun directly (that is, without burning our eyes).
Instead, as one early Christian mystic, Meister Eckhart, put it, we
learn to 'penetrate everything and find the God within.' Similarly,
Goethe wrote of 'God's presence in each element.'"

Maureen stopped me, saying:

> Wait, let me copy down your three God-images. If I moved from
> picture number 1 to picture number 3, then it seems as though
> I haven't made a long detour in my spiritual life. Instead, I feel
> that all the time I was focusing on Saul, the children, my work,
> or the community, I was seeing the world illuminated by God,
> because I couldn't take the intensity of looking at God directly.
> But I felt the deadness.

"And the deadness must be addressed," I said, "but not by a return
to a frightening, less mature God-image. To see God in and through
everything around us is *not* to see an ordinary or boring event. It is to
be open to wonder, even awe—but not an awe that is life-denying.
Where was God when your daughter was born? Tell me more about
those so-called years in the house of Laban."

Maureen asked what that expression meant. I recounted the biblical tale:

"Jacob flees his parents' home and en route to Paddan-aran, he has the awesome vision of a ladder joining heaven and earth. He then spends the next twenty years in the house of Laban, falling in love with his daughters, marrying, and fathering twelve sons and a daughter. But only after he leaves Laban does he have another vision."

"Oh, right," said Maureen,

> that's wonderful. I never liked Jacob—but I see what you mean. He stole Esau's blessing and really was a "heel" (the Hebrew name for Jacob even means "heel"!) when he fled to Paddan-aran—but raising a family tempered him and made him more ready for his next encounter with God. So you're really saying that my conversion, marriage, and family were not detours on the way, they were the way itself. I still had this involuntary longing for a spiritual life that I envisioned in extremes: going off to the Himalayas or off to the desert or a monastery—well, I guess a convent would have been more appropriate.

At this point I opened my *Tanach* to one of my favorite passages in Deuteronomy 30:12–14:

> It is not in the heavens that you should say, "Who among us can go up to the heavens and get it for us and impart it to us that we may observe it?" Neither is it beyond the sea, that you should say, "Who among us can cross to the other side of the sea and get it for us and impart it to us, that we may observe it?" No, the thing is very close to you, in your mouth and in your heart, to observe it.

"Can you give me chapter and verse of the Deuteronomy quotation?" Maureen asked.

> You've given me a lot to think about. I want to study those God-images you drew, and the quotes you gave me from Goethe and, who was it, Eckhart? I came here thinking I had made a long detour—I didn't feel as if I had, but I thought I had. I have a lot of work to do before I see you again.

Afterword

A number of years have passed since I worked with the individuals discussed in this book. I have not deliberately done follow-ups, but I do know where many of them are now and what they are doing. Some have kept me posted, others sent regards through third parties, and one is back in touch after a lapse of many years. I am always interested to learn how our time together fed into other aspects of their lives. And although I can never fully know that, I do know how working with them has fed into *my* life.

Through all the years that I have served as a spiritual guide, I have also been in spiritual guidance. I require that of myself, much as teachers and nurses are required to take continuing-education units. I use the sessions both to examine my own spiritual growth and to have a sounding board for my own work with guidees. Through these sessions I have become aware that serving as a spiritual guide has been my most significant spiritual practice. It has been intense and challenging, stretching me to the limit of what I can understand. Also, it has given me a place where I can talk about God unashamedly, marvel at the diversity of people's stories, and recognize how often we are helped to exceed what we feel capable of doing.

While in high school, I sang with the Renaissance Chorus of New York, which performed only works composed before 1600. The music was written largely without accidentals, signs that make a note one-half step higher or lower. Such accidentals—sharps and flats— were meant to be added by the performers, a Renaissance practice called applying *musica ficta* (literally, "false music"). One year, we began rehearsals of a fifteenth-century Mass composed by Josquin Desprez and based on a song of the time, "Une musque de Biscaye" (A maid of Biscay). Since no one could reliably say how to apply the *musica ficta* to this work, the job fell to our conductor, Harold Brown. Brown began assigning accidentals to the first movement very tentatively, fearing that he might not be following the composer's intentions. By the time he got to the last movement, though, all uncertainty was gone. His long work over the first five movements had given him a feel for the music that he had lacked at the start. I see something like that same growth in assurance over my years as a spiritual guide. Early on, I hesitated to point out to my guidees the surprising and daring ways in which God is revealed in each story. I am still filled with wonder and awe, but I feel much more at ease in allowing myself to react to a guidee's story.

The cases set out here exhibit just a taste of the dizzying variety of ways in which God can come to us. Yet, even with all the celebration of our uniqueness, certain patterns keep reappearing. Perhaps the first landmark I see in guidees is an awakening to the reality of their souls. When I mention "soul," I do not mean some supersensible organ that might be hidden in a part of our brains or even our hearts. Belief in the soul is simply a belief that the world is more than all we see, hear, and touch. We all know the difference between appearance and reality, but we rarely apply it to ourselves. The Psalmist can say, "The stone that the builders rejected has become the chief cornerstone" (Psalm 118:22), but how do we recognize the part of ourselves that no one else can see or know? The twentieth-century analytic philosopher Ludwig Wittgenstein wrote, "The world is everything that is the case." That sounds fairly obvious, almost tautological. But for those who have awakened to the reality of their souls, the statement not only is not a tautology, it is false! The world is everything that is the case and more, and it is the "more" that spells out the meaning of soul. The world is everything that once was the case and that could be the case, and it is *our relationship to what is the case.*

We learn that for God, all of time is present: past, present, and future coexist. We, in the image of God, find ourselves living in the present but with the sense of wonder we gained as our younger selves and the sense of insight and adventure of our future selves. Our lives are part of a larger pattern, and only by incorporating all of time can we get flashes, now and then, of the whole to which we contribute. "What should be the case" reminds us that those who awaken to the reality of their souls increase their commitment to this world and feel an urge to help heal the world's brokenness. That is because at every stage on the spiritual way, we recall that we are not our own end. The journey is richly satisfying, but we pursue it because we grow in love with God and with God's creations.

Awakening to the reality of the soul makes us more aware of both the beauty and the sordidness of the world. We feel an almost prophetic moral outrage at how this magnificent creation can have been led so far off course. But we also acquire a deep sense of tranquility and peace. In this paradoxical combination of anger and calm, we are given both the disease and the cure. We perceive what needs to be done, and we feel a quiet assurance that we can do it because we are not alone. And that belief fosters our appreciation of what we have received. The comment at the end of the days of Creation in Genesis, "And God saw that it was good," becomes viscerally true for us.

Further, we feel an increasing connectedness of all things and a lessening of fear, which loosens all our boundaries. Overall, we may remember how we felt when we realized we were in love. It wasn't only the beloved that was beautiful, it was the whole world of our loved one. When had we ever been so open and appreciative to the sweet sound of birds, the ineffable perfume of flowers, the brilliant shaft of light breaking through the clouds? Because the spiritual way is the way of love, we should not be surprised that an important landmark on the spiritual way should produce the same feelings we experience in our human love relationships. It also follows that spiritual guidance resembles psychotherapy less than it resembles marriage counseling. It is all about a deepening relationship between the seeker and God, and it is the guide's job to facilitate the relationship while staying as much as possible out of the way.

When I first fell in love, I was not sure of what was happening. Others had to point out that my interests and behaviors suggested that I was in love. They even had to show me that the wonderful things that were happening in my life did not result from chance or luck, but were the gracious gift of one who loved me. There came a period of exquisite shyness, when I could not bring myself to say my beloved's name, only to be followed by a period in which I couldn't find enough excuses for all the times I pronounced it. And all of these patterns, so painfully formed in my first love relationship, play out again in my love of God.

Now, as I see daily the love awakening and growing in the lives of my guidees, I am less tentative in "applying the *musica ficta*" to their stories—that is, helping them recognize the real meanings and goodness in their lives and the source of that goodness. When they say "luck" or "good fortune," I remind them that luck and good fortune are names of pagan gods. Why not turn to the real source?

As in marriage counseling, my guidees must be convinced that their beloved is not simply an extension of themselves, but is other and should be loved and appreciated in otherness, not reduced to the one who meets their needs. Just as children first love their parents for meeting all their desires and later try to apply a similar standard for their life partners, so we tend to judge God in terms of our needs and wishes. Gradually, we come to recognize that our parents are people with a whole life history themselves, and we love them for who they are, not who they are for us. Something analogous can happen in our relationship to a partner. And, finally, at some point, we love God not for God's gifts but for God's self. We are reminded of the coexistence of all time. Here we are as adults, drawn back to the neediness of young children, and yet, together, we work so that the future, which already exists within, can be born.

Again as in marriage counseling, guidees must learn to express anger as a form of communication, a difficult task when the anger is directed at God. First, the guidees must recognize and claim the anger, which they rationally believe to be unwarranted. Nevertheless they feel it, and the anger obstructs a deeper relationship with God. But even after recognizing the anger, it can be very difficult to learn how to express it so that it promotes some healing.

Healing has two major prerequisites: a sense of safety—or, at least, an absence of threat—and an abundance of love. Feeling safe requires us to recall where God was during major turning points in our lives. And because the present projects back to the past and forward into the future, our relationship with God takes us back to our own experiences and brings us forward to our own commitment. On three occasions, I have heard people on their deathbeds ask themselves, "Can I trust God?" There, with no known outcome ahead except death, the people could recall and savor the goodness of life and their own sense of safety in God's faithful care. These same exercises in memory and reflection frequently allow people to grasp the fact that they are loved, appreciated, accepted—even welcomed. I have seen this insight occur, and it carries the transformative power of finally convincing the individuals that they are loved.

We are called to ever-deepening love, commitment, and intimacy with God. The journey is unending, and we are always beginners. I have been privileged to share much of my journey with fellow seekers, who have given me the chance to hear their stories and accompany them for part of their way. I awaken each morning with the joyous realization that the adventure need never end.